Making the Jump

into Small Business Ownership

David Nilssen and Jeff Levy

BOOK PUBLISHERS NETWORK

Book Publishers Network
P.O. Box 2256
Bothell • WA • 98041
Ph • 425-483-3040
www.bookpublishersnetwork.com

10 9 8 7 6 5 4 3 2 1

Printed in the United States of America

LCCN 2011907089
ISBN10 1-935359-83-5
ISBN13 978-1-935359-83-8

Editor: Kathleen Florio
Cover Designer: Laura Zugzda
Typographer: Stephanie Martindale

Disclaimer: This book is based upon the practical knowledge and experience of the authors. It is not meant to be a technical manual on all elements of starting a business. You are encouraged to seek the help of professionals such as an attorney, an accountant, a business broker, a banker, a coach, and others when making final decisions.

We dedicate this book to those who had the courage to "make the jump" into small business ownership. Entrepreneurs solve the world's greatest challenges, stimulate the economy, create jobs, and preserve the qualities that have made the United States the greatest country on earth.

Contents

Acknowledgments

This is the first book for both of us; we had no idea what we had committed ourselves to. Throughout the process we learned that it truly takes a village to write a book.

We will be forever grateful to the many people we asked to donate their time, on weekends, at night, and away from their family to ensure the final product was what we wanted. These individuals include, but are not limited to, Kathleen Florio, Andrea Levy, Brian Miller, Stephen Holmes, Dan Parker, Steve Brilling, Lorinda Church, Sara Spencer, Jeremy Ames, Nicole Cox, Drew Bruns, Mindee Nodvin, Sharon Peterson, Ralph Nilssen, Patti Nilssen, Michael Burke, and Lori Kiser-Block. We appreciate the thoroughness with which they reviewed the manuscripts and then with great sensitivity told us we still had a lot of work to do. Lastly, we want to thank the entrepreneurs who allowed us to use their stories and experiences, allowing our readers to learn from them. It is the small-business owner, the franchisee, the entrepreneur—like you—who inspires us every day. Thank you!

Introduction

The economic meltdown of 2008 was a wake-up call for anyone who assumes that a career in corporate America is secure. The painful lesson learned by a significant portion of America's workforce was this: If you work for someone else, you have little control over your employment status and are investing in that person's dream, not your own.

In 2010, the unemployment rate of America's workers rose about 10 percent. We wrote this book in response to a deep need we saw for people to discover the benefits of self-reliance. In our humble opinion, there is no greater vehicle for security than owning your own business. When successful, a business can defy most financial models and calculations. While 2010 has come and gone, the need is still real and will live on.

The reasons to go into business for yourself are infinite. Perhaps you want to spend more time with your family. Maybe you want to earn more income, call the shots, or travel more often. Is there something you enjoy doing more than anything else—and can you earn an income doing so? Regardless of your motivation, the answer to the question "Should I go into business for myself" is yes. Small business ownership can be a path to true independence, life balance, and personal happiness.

About This Book

As successful entrepreneurs, we have identified significant opportunities and assumed many risks, and ultimately chose to pursue our dreams. Because there are over 30 years separating us in age, our book covers generational as well as universal perspectives and insights.

Our goal is to present in these pages a practical guide on how to build self-reliance and start your own business. We will speak to the fundamentals, the block and tackle, of entrepreneurship, and we will address the challenges that most new entrepreneurs face. In several of the chapters you will find vignettes—stories of real-life entrepreneurs whose experiences illustrate some of our main points. We hope you will find their stories inspiring as well as informative.

This book is *not* about deal junkies and their seemingly magical ventures that start on a short runway and take off with sales that seem to defy gravity. We are not addressing "vaporware" or unprofitable companies that go public and return a gazillion dollars—before imploding. Like winning the lottery, these successes represent only a small slice of start-up ventures.

We firmly believe that the future security and prosperity of baby boomers and new college graduates—and all the generations in between—will be reached by encouraging entrepreneurship based upon sound business principles. Small businesses, and the entrepreneurs who start them, create more than 50 percent of American jobs. By encouraging displaced workers and others to become entrepreneurs and expand this important sector of the economic base, we hope to add new fuel to the American small-business growth engine—and perhaps power your dreams in the process.

About the Authors

So why should you care what we—David Nilssen and Jeff Levy—have to say about entrepreneurship and launching a small business? You should care because both of us started with little to nothing and now we are living our dreams of not only running successful enterprises but helping others launch their own businesses. We have faced the tough times, and we have certainly made our mistakes ... yet we persevered and overcame those challenges. Does this mean we're no longer making mistakes or crashing headfirst into brick walls? Absolutely not! The bumps and bruises are a natural part of starting and running a business. But as experienced entrepreneurs, we know how to avoid some of the largest obstacles and how to recover in a hurry. And this is what we'll teach you to do, too. When we want to share a particularly important piece of information from personal experience, we'll convey it in an insert titled "From the desk of ..."

Neither of us has an advanced degree in finance or business, yet each of us has owned and successfully operated multiple small businesses and have experience helping to build partnerships and family businesses. This, in itself, should encourage those of you who fear your lack of academic credentials could interfere with your success!

So how did we get to this point? Here, in our own words, are our personal stories.

From the Desk of David Nilssen

Along with my parents, two brothers, and two sisters, I grew up in the small town of Maple Valley, Washington. Life was simple, "normal." In school I pursued leadership positions, played sports, and got good grades. My father was the president of an international Christmas tree company (and yes, they work all year round!). He was an ambitious operator (who later bought the company from the owners) who, by example, taught me a lot about work-life balance.

Growing up I was a sports fanatic—and at six foot five, I was pretty successful as a shooting guard. What I learned from an early age was that basketball, like any team sport, is as much mental as it is physical. To win, you must put the right players in positions in which they can excel. The coach must have the right strategy, and you, the player, must execute with the utmost discipline. Achieving success in business comes through the same attributes and hard work that allow athletes to be great. There are a lot of parallels in sports and business. I didn't realize that until starting a land-development business at the age of 23.

Fast forward to today. I am the cofounder of a company that helps aspiring entrepreneurs successfully invest in or finance a business. At the time of this writing, our company had helped more than 5,000 individuals, in all 50 states, deploy more than $2 billion to purchase a small business or franchise. We estimate that to date, our clients have created 50,000-plus jobs. We have empowered individuals to pursue their own American dream through small business ownership. I love what I do—and I want you to love what you do, too.

From the Desk of Jeff Levy

Over the course of 40 years, I have been recognized nationally as a business consultant. I am closer to five foot six, and sports were not my guide as they were for my writing partner. What I learned later in life was that to be successful, you needed to own something and through your efforts grow that asset; and that motivation came through quality-of-life goals that I was passionate about.

Today I am a client-focused mentor, and as a business coaching franchisee, I am working with approximately 250 different franchise businesses. I match franchises to individuals based on their objectives. I have personally coached more than 100 individuals who have become franchisees. In my prior work, I was president and COO of Spider Staging before the acquisition of the enterprise by Flow International in 1992. I served as an officer at Flow, a public company, for five years until a partner and I developed a management buyout of several Flow divisions. I then became the executive vice president and a principle of SafeWorks LLC. I sold my interests in Safeworks in 2002, when I moved into consulting with prospective franchisees.

A Hard Truth

Much of corporate America has proven itself to be obsessed with profit. Relying on corporate giants for dependable salaries and benefits is a gamble at best. And to expect any employer—large or small—to provide us retirement benefits to support our long-term needs is nothing short of naïve.

Part of the problem relates to major restructuring in the US economy, including the end of manufacturing as the dominant sector, the impact of technology in lowering the costs of labor, and the effects of globalization. The labor pool has become highly competitive as the benefit of outsourcing jobs internationally has created significant challenges for our domestic workers. While the cost of living has stalled, a majority of those fortunate enough to have steady jobs during the first decade of the 21st century have discovered that a salary is often insufficient to keep up with the ever-rising US standard of living. According to CreditCards.com (www.creditcards.com), the average credit card debt per household was $15,788, while My Budget 360 (www.mybudget360.com) reported the median household income to be just $52,000. These figures suggest that the average employee is not capable of accumulating the cash and assets necessary to retire wealthy.

There is, however, one route we have found to be the most promising path to financial security and the happiness and wealth that comes with it: *Take control of your future by investing in your own business.*

During our careers, the two of us have interacted with hundreds of men and women in every age group, economic strata, employed and in transition, and with varying degrees of education and economic status. We call them "entrepreneurial dreamers" because they all ask the question: "What if I was my own boss?"

Their common bond was that they were ready to test the waters of self-reliance. For some reason—perhaps a recent lay-off or something they read in a self-help or business book—they sat down with a mentor or business coach and decided they were not willing to defer their dream of self-employment any longer. Their belief was that having a corporate career until retirement was just not going to be enough.

The ability to make one's own choices starts and is motivated by a dream; a "what if" scenario in which individuals begin to want their life to be different than it was before. The famous quote "Life isn't about finding yourself. Life is about creating yourself," George Bernard Shaw, speaks to the heart of the entrepreneurial dream. These dreamers have a great desire to make something in their life, or the lives of others, better. Where do these roots come from?

Do you remember your childhood ideas of the future? What did you want to be when you grew up? Why? How many times did this change?

Many entrepreneurial motivations can be traced back as far as childhood. Some entrepreneurs received recognition and encouragement as children, which gave them confidence and knowledge. Other entrepreneurs look back on childhoods of poverty and neglect, and it's those circumstances that drove them to succeed.

What, then, differentiates those who will face the risks and become entrepreneurs and those who simply admire them, dreaming of taking the plunge yet clinging tightly to the towrope of employment that pulls them along?

Successful entrepreneurship is often attributed to confidence. But how can one attain confidence? Prescribing confidence seems as abstract as stipulating immortality.

While it's absolutely true that confidence is a prerequisite for moving forward as an entrepreneur, sometimes it involves adjusting your beliefs. As Wayne Dyer says, "Look at the world from a perspective of infinite opportunity and not scarcity."

True confidence is not manifested by mantras of self-praise or repetitive chanting of "I think I can"; instead it is manifested by the very fundamental principles of a driven existence:

- In risk is reward.
- In fear is adrenaline.
- In optimism is energy.
- In self-development is self-reliance.
- In change is growth.
- In failure is success.
- In winter are the seeds of spring.

Now ... About You

If you are reading this book, it's likely you already have a solid entrepreneurial vision and you're willing to work hard to build a business around it. If *you* bring the initiative and motivation, then *we* will provide the tools to help you launch your entrepreneurial future!

Section I:
Find the Entrepreneur in You

The Entrepreneur Versus the Employee

"In the long run, we shape our lives, and we shape ourselves. The process never ends until we die. And the choices we make are ultimately our own responsibility."

—Eleanor Roosevelt

What is the attraction? Why are so many people enamored with the idea of owning a small business? You make your own hours; work with whomever you want; make tons of money. Sounds like a dream, doesn't it? While all of these benefits are possible, entrepreneurship is neither simple nor easy. If it were, everyone would be doing it.

The Employee

Many employees dream of being "the boss." Yet business brokers and franchisors estimate that as many as 70 percent of the people who come to them to learn about buying a business will neither buy nor start a business. So most employees dream of owning a business but will never implement their dream. What holds them back? For many, the answer is fear. Many employees are motivated to stay where they are by the perception of safety a regular job seems to offer. While a guaranteed salary, health insurance, job training, and potential cash bonuses are all possible benefits of working for an employer, many employees do not understand the risks they assume every day, such as getting fired or having the company they work for be downsized.

There was a time when many jobs *did* offer security. It used to be that we would graduate from school and then find employment with a company and stay there for most, if not all, of our career. In return for our hard work and loyalty, our employer would provide us a defined benefit—a pension. Those days are gone. Then in 1974, Congress passed ERISA, the Employee Retirement Income Security Act, which created defined contribution plans such as IRAs and 401(k)s and ultimately shifted the responsibility for retirement funding from the employer to the employee—you.

Nowadays, with mergers, layoffs, company relocations, and the changes associated with a global economy, the average employee is expected to have 10 different employers throughout his or her career and to make at least one complete career change. Often employees are not rewarded for exceptional performance and can be dismissed at any time without notice. Budget considerations often override the provision of incentives. Seems there is really little security in working for others!

In addition to the overall lack of job security, most employment offers little or no control over the amount of the paycheck. Once people are hired, they make the same pay week in and week out, with perhaps a small annual adjustment to "cover" the increase in cost of living.

Despite all these drawbacks, most employees are afraid to take the risks associated with not having a weekly paycheck, and they fear the unknown of business ownership. The twin demons of risk and fear are so significant, we devote an entire chapter to them (see Chapter 12). But for now, consider the following Webster's dictionary definition of *fear*:

> *Fear*—to be afraid or to feel anxious about a possible situation or event

The definition of *fear* all but says that fear is attributable to a lack of knowledge. Thus it is reasonable to assume that the way to eliminate fear of the unknown is to become informed. Knowledge instills confidence, and experience enhances assurance. Learning about start-ups, business acquisition, and franchise awards will give you confidence while you explore entrepreneurship. Today, entrepreneur clubs, organizations, certificate programs at colleges and universities, and counselors at SCORE and Small Business Development Centers (SBDCs) and other such organizations can be helpful in overcoming fear.

And it could be that exploring entrepreneurship will become an increasingly common undertaking. The *Wall Street Journal* recently reported that today's college graduates see self-employment and getting a job as providing an equivalent amount of security. That view represents quite a paradigm shift from only a decade or two ago. Keep in mind, too, what Thomas Friedman of the *New York Times* wrote in his book *The World Is Flat*: "A flat world is one in which the individual worker is going to become more and more responsible for managing his or her own career, risks, and economic security...."

Environment and Influence

Often the people around us are not the most productive influences for the pursuit of our entrepreneurial dreams. Negative statements are sometimes spurred by jealousy from people who are afraid to follow their own dreams.

For every entrepreneurial dreamer, there is someone who says, "You can't do that," "That will never work," or otherwise expresses pessimism. To those folks, we say, "Get out of the way." Successful entrepreneurs have the ability to choose who and what they will allow to affect them and how they will respond. They limit negative influences and replace them with sources of encouragement and affirmation.

If you choose to open and operate a small business, you may have to change your circle of influence. One of the best things you can do is surround yourself with successful, positive, and supportive people who will help you undertake this new journey. If you want to find other people like you, there are many organizations that provide peer-to-peer learning for business owners and entrepreneurs, such as the Entrepreneurs' Organization (http:// www.eonetwork.org) and Vistage (www.vistage.com). In addition, many universities and community colleges have resources such as Entrepreneurship Centers to support start-up businesses. (See also Chapter 3, which discusses mentors.)

But before we get too far ahead of ourselves, let's get to the basic question: *Do you have what it takes to be an entrepreneur?*

As you read through the following sections, take the time to check in periodically with yourself and honestly evaluate whether you have the personality, the drive, and the skills that would make you a successful entrepreneur.

Are You an Entrepreneur?

Owning a business is exciting and fulfilling, and can provide benefits that greatly exceed working for a wage or salary. But it's not easy. In fact, entrepreneurship requires a big sacrifice and demands serious, thoughtful consideration. Here are some questions you should ask yourself if you are considering jumping into the world of entrepreneurship:

- Can you go without a paycheck for 6 to 24 months?
- Are you capable of putting a vision ahead of your short-term needs?
- Do you perform well under pressure?
- Are you a strong mentor or coach?
- Are you a decisive person?

- Will your family be able to support this decision knowing you will likely have to work longer hours and face initial financial insecurity?

- Are you a self-starter?

- Have you been able to work independently, without close supervision?

- Are you responsible and accountable at all times?

To be a successful entrepreneur, you should be able to honestly and confidently answer these questions (and others!) with a "yes."

General Characteristics of an Entrepreneur

Through our own experience of owning and managing companies, and having helped coach thousands of entrepreneurs, we have noticed a mindset—common personality traits and behaviors—in people who become successful small-business owners. (To put this in perspective, we should make clear that we are not talking here about CEOs of major enterprises, who often can be seen as ego driven, abrupt, and impatient, focused primarily on the value of their publicly traded stock. There are always extremes.) But our collective view is that small-business owners need to set the personality and culture of their organization. While managing employees, we've recognized certain entrepreneurial qualities in those who were motivated by the desire for eventual independence—to someday sign the *front* of the check rather than the back! Here are the qualities that suggest a propensity for successful entrepreneurship.

Attention to Details. When starting a new venture, it is human nature to do what we *like* to do rather than what we *have* to do. But the old adage "the devil is in the details" does apply to budding entrepreneurs. While vision and strategy are critical to success, it's also important to make sure the fundamentals such as accounting and cash management are addressed, and general attention is given to the smaller decisions as well. Even though business gurus like Michael Gerber encourage you to be the visionary and not the technician or the manager, someone needs to be assigned the lesser but significant task of minding the details. Until you build staff, that responsibility will likely fall to you.

Balanced Optimism. Successful entrepreneurs have what we like to call "balanced optimism." They believe they will realize a successful outcome because they have collected adequate information and eliminated most fear. They are not so naïve as to think that everything will always go smoothly, but they arm themselves with enough data to be comfortable in their decisions.

They also exhibit a contagious enthusiasm and often a charisma that attracts people to them. They expect and look for the best in others.

Competitiveness. Entrepreneurs love winning. They see challenge as the journey and enjoy the victory as much as—or even more than—the actual reward. To use a sports metaphor: *Winning is the goal, and money is often seen as the score.*

Decisiveness/Accountability. While most employees will look for someone else to make a decision so they know whom to blame, entrepreneurs are comfortable making decisions and owning the outcome. Thriving entrepreneurs are accountable for their actions and decisions and for the effectiveness of their business. They do not hide their mistakes but admit and learn from them. This accountability strengthens their decision-making ability. When they are honest with themselves and their perspective isn't clouded by ego or defensiveness, they are more likely to see situations clearly, so they can realistically identify challenges and opportunities. They consider their customers' responses and their employees' satisfaction and performance as measuring sticks of their own performance. Successful entrepreneurs are comfortable with accountability and responsibility; they don't simply attribute their success or failure to things that are beyond their control.

Decisiveness and accountability are often taught or acquired at an early stage and should guide your career choices. When you are willing to take responsibility for your actions, decisions, and behavior, and as you practice this assumption of responsibility, you reduce the fear of taking action because you consider the consequences beforehand, and that in turn helps you make better decisions. If you are willing to take responsibility, assuming your skills and experience are up to the task, why not become the boss?

Fear of Mediocrity. Entrepreneurs cannot tolerate mediocrity or failure. Success is the only result acceptable to them, and they will work hard to meet their goals. Ironically, many entrepreneurs define their past failures as successes because they perceive failure as a learning experience. This ability to "see the glass as half full" enables them to persist. They do not define themselves by their failures but by the knowledge and wisdom they gain.

Flexibility. By the very nature of their work, entrepreneurs are required to perform many tasks. They can multitask and change hats quickly. They also are ready and willing to adapt their plans to the challenges on hand and to embrace the changes needed to reach their goals.

Great Communication Skills. In this case, we are not referring to good speaking and listening skills, although, of course, those are necessary leadership traits. We are speaking of the ability to share one's vision and create excitement. Because they believe deeply in their cause, true entrepreneurs can generate enthusiasm in others.

New business owners sometimes have trouble accepting the fact that their employees are not driven by the same inner motivation to succeed. Many times they fail to realize the importance of giving their employees something to be excited about, and therefore they do not properly motivate their own employees. Yet all successful entrepreneurs learn to motivate their teams by communicating their business (and often personal) visions and goals. This ability to communicate their passion follows them into the hiring process so they can surround themselves with employees who are also passionate and share the same goals.

Hard-Work Ethic. Successful entrepreneurs have a strong work ethic and understand that time is their scarcest resource. This does not mean they try to outwork everyone; they simply do whatever it takes to get the job done, and they usually operate at a high efficiency level.

Imagination. People who have the potential to make it on their own—and in a big way—are extremely creative. They recognize that the best solutions are rarely found within the status quo. So they come up with unique ideas for products, services, advertising, marketing, and even the most practical aspects of the job. Potential solutions continually come to mind in bursts of creativity, like popcorn. They can take one bit of information, see its potential, and come up with imaginative ways to make it work to serve their own needs, wants, and goals.

Independence. Successful entrepreneurship is dependent on leadership skills that grow out of the ability to work independently and trust one's own judgment. But "independent" does not mean "in isolation." Entrepreneurs seek out mentors and coaches, keep an open mind, listen to advice, quickly absorb new information, and implement new processes when needed. They attract others with their confidence and energy.

Introspectiveness. The best entrepreneurs have a very good sense of self and a great understanding of their strengths and weaknesses, and they build teams to balance their deficiencies. This sense of self is developed by the belief in, and desire for, self-improvement. Some entrepreneurs are so driven, they tend to judge themselves too harshly. Truly successful (and happy) entrepreneurs have learned to balance their self-criticism with an open and realistic look at their many accomplishments.

Maniacal Focus. With their "eyes on the prize," entrepreneurs stay the course and are tenaciously persistent. They often perform best in the face of adversity and are motivated, not deterred, by the obstacles in their path.

Self-Confidence. Entrepreneurs believe strongly in their skills and abilities, allowing them to calculate risks to a comfortable level. They use a "gut feeling"—combined with good knowledge—to guide their decisions, and they are willing to "bet the store" on their choices. They strive to maintain absolute control over their destinies.

As employees, most future entrepreneurs are frustrated by the slower pace, inefficiencies, and politics of a job or their employer. Because they trust themselves more, and usually have (or have gained) more business knowledge than other employees, they often become entrepreneurs and exit the employment arena out of frustration.

 From the Desk of David Nilssen

One of my greatest mentors is a man named Dave Parker, an accomplished entrepreneur whom I met in 2004. One of the greatest pieces of advice he gave me was this: "Trust your gut. It will seldom lead you in the wrong direction."

I have repeated this quote many times to staff, partners, friends, clients, and even my family. There are many studies that confirm that good decisions can often be made without any deliberation. If you are operating with good information and under no extraneous pressure, your gut is seldom wrong. Trust it.

Many successful entrepreneurs attribute successes to gut instinct—the voice within us that is often shaped by an accumulation of knowledge gained from experience, skills practice, trial and error, and decision making. A sports anecdote illustrates the point. An aspiring young baseball player was working hard at his swing. He analyzed his stance, how high he held the bat, and his alignment with the plate, and he drew pictures of each angle of his body. By chance, he was hired to work a charity baseball game. Before the game his group was gathered on the field while the team was warming up, and a baseball rolled to his feet. He picked up the ball, turned around, and was astonished to see his idol, Babe Ruth, in person, holding out his hand. Without hesitation the young athlete blurted out, "Mr. Ruth, how do you know how to hold the bat and at what angle to swing?" The Babe paused and responded, "Son, I haven't thought about that in years. I just hit the ball."

Self-Discipline. Successful entrepreneurs practice self-discipline. They apply strong work ethics and adhere to their standards. Because they have vision, they realize their sacrifices and efforts will be rewarded—if not immediately, then in the future.

Self-Motivation. Although entrepreneurs' motivation will vary, the intensity is usually on the high end of the barometer. They are fiercely driven and continually measure their successes against their goals. Successful entrepreneurs do not wait for someone to give them permission to get started. They are activators—hard-driving and energetic people who seize opportunity whenever they see it.

Successful entrepreneurs are fully dedicated to their business and will work hard to realize their goals and dreams. They are remarkably persistent. While they fully understand that achieving and maintaining success can be difficult, they are ready to meet the challenges head-on. They know even before they start out that reaching goals often requires extreme amounts of time, effort, and unstinting dedication, but they do not let this deter them from reaching for their vision.

Sense of Urgency. Entrepreneurs work with a sense of urgency. They understand the value of time, and they work with intention. They understand the consequences of delayed action or inaction, and they know tomorrow may be too late.

Tenacity. True entrepreneurs view failures as temporary. When facing obstacles, entrepreneurs find a way to overcome them. They use mistakes and errors to become better at what they do instead of falling prey to discouragement and doubt. They have a remarkable talent for recognizing their personal or business weaknesses and an unflagging ability to overcome them.

Vision. Entrepreneurs have defined dreams. They have big plans and think from a 30,000-foot perspective. Many of them visualize themselves in the future. They can tell you exactly how they see themselves in their business in the future.

Willingness to Sacrifice. Entrepreneurs are willing to make great sacrifices to achieve success. Often they will sacrifice many things most employees would never dream of giving up. Their drive and goals are more important than the routine self-gratification associated with simple entertainment. Their pursuits become their gratification.

✳ ✳ ✳

To be completely fair, you likely are not great in each of these areas. Even if you don't have all of these characteristics, however, do not worry. Many of them can be learned or improved upon, especially if you set goals to do so.

Now that you have an idea of the qualities associated with being an entrepreneur, you may still wonder whether you are suited to be a small-business owner—which involves some additional important considerations. The good news is that the answer can be found within the individual who poses the question. No one can make this determination for you. Entrepreneurism is a realistic path to achieving your dreams; and achieving your goal begins with a set of explorations that should come before an attempt is made to start or buy a business. We call it "pre-work," and it includes a personal inventory of strengths and areas for improvement, introspection, candid self-evaluation, and above all else, a sense of clarity regarding your financial, lifestyle, and personal objectives.

Being an entrepreneur is not for everyone. But armed with an organized approach to understanding your skills and objectives, you'll find that there are definitely opportunities to be the conductor rather than the second fiddle. The next chapter offers some specific suggestions for beginning the transition.

From Employee to Entrepreneur: Dulcee's Story

Sometimes it takes more than just the allure of being one's own boss to inspire one to start a business; it takes finding a business or franchise that truly matches one's passions. For people with years of business experience who want to make the transition from employee to entrepreneur, starting a business-coaching franchise might be an excellent option.

Dulcee was itching to have her own business for more than two years before she started a coaching franchise. She could not have guessed where her experiences would take her. Her academic background was in biology, and after college she had worked at a small laboratory-supply company that was owned by a married couple. The husband handled outside sales; the wife handled almost everything inside, but her passion was tennis, and so Dulcee was soon assuming most of the responsibilities in the office.

Dulcee recalls, "I learned every aspect of how to run a small business, … from inside sales to accounts receivable, to accounts payable, to customer service, to shipping." This was extremely useful experience and a good venue for her skills, but her passions lay elsewhere.

She then spent over 10 years in the corporate world, working in middle management and higher up, and eventually coaching other managers. For nine years, she worked at Johnson Controls, a building controls and HVAC service provider, where she tracked performance indicators for the state of Florida and Puerto Rico.

But her role went beyond analysis. Dulcee explains: "I worked with the managers who had the P&L responsibility for their business. I would help them maximize their key performance indicators and reach or exceed their goals. I really was a coach, although I didn't call it that at the time. We'd look at every aspect of their business, and how to grow their business, become more effective and efficient and decrease their costs."

Over time, she began to recognize that she loved looking at a business—in her words—as if it were "a machine, and getting that machine running at an optimum level." This prompted her to pursue an advanced degree; but rather than seeking an MBA, which she felt would teach her little that she did not already know from experience, she began a program at the University of South Florida for a master's degree in Management Leadership and Organizational Effectiveness, and completed it in 2006.

Business coaching as a career combines the two things that she most enjoys: optimizing business and helping people. "Those are the two things I really enjoy. I wasn't a big fan of the politics in the corporate world. I really didn't want to go back to that," she says.

Dulcee shares in her clients' successes and enjoys her own, though she admits that owning a small business is a lot of work. "I've never worked harder in my life—and I thought I worked hard before—but now I'm working for myself. I don't have anywhere near the stress level that I used to have." Much of that is the result of simply taking charge of her time and being recognized for her accomplishments. "I control how much money I make; I control how many hours I work; I control how much stress is in my life. … I jump out of bed in the morning excited to get started, which I honestly admit was just not the case before."

Careful due diligence and efficiency are key factors in her success, but she has two more bits of advice for small-business owners and people who are considering starting a small business or franchise: "Make sure that you're passionate about it because you're going to spend a lot of time doing it. Secondly, be prepared to put all of your energy into it for a while, because it takes time to build a business."

Do You Have What It Takes to Run a Business?

In this chapter we'll help you take a closer look at whether you have the traits and skills required to run a successful business. Begin by asking yourself the following questions—and if too many of your answers are "no," it could be that you have an entrepreneurial drive but not the skills or disposition to plunge headfirst into actually running a business.

- Are you self-motivated, and do you look at the world as being full of opportunity?

- Are you organized?

- Can you operate with intent?

- Are you proficient at the key business disciplines: vision, management, finance, accounting, marketing, sales, information management (IT), and customer service? If not, can you develop a team to complement your talents?

- Can you admit to what you do not know?

- Are you willing to grow in the areas required and put your business before yourself?

- Do you believe there is a relationship between risk and reward?

- If you're interested in running a franchise, can you set aside old habits and beliefs to follow a system developed by someone else?

Reality Check: Entrepreneurial Pros and Cons

Even if you think you've got the personal qualities and traits to be an entrepreneur, and even if your answers to the preceding questions suggest that you've got what it takes to run a business, you should be well aware of the plusses and minuses of entrepreneurship. Based on our personal experiences, and those of the many we have coached, we've found many pros and cons that are directly related to being an entrepreneur.

The advantages include the following:

- Freedom and independence

- Control over a major aspect of your life

- Outlet for creativity

- Excitement

- Satisfaction and sense of achievement

- Self-esteem

- Status and recognition

- Flexibility

- Job security: you can't be fired or laid off

- No cap on income potential

- Growth of initial investment

The disadvantages include the following:

- Risk, responsibility, and pressure

- Fear of failure

- Obstacles and frustration
- Loneliness
- More work, longer hours
- Less time or energy to spend with friends and family
- Less financial security to start with
- Fewer job benefits
- Risk of losing investment
- Income fluctuation
- Responsibility for taxes, Social Security

True entrepreneurs embrace the risks because of their belief that there is more to gain. After reviewing these pros and cons, how do you feel? Are you still enthusiastic about becoming an entrepreneur?

Business Skills

Enthusiasm is important, but in the real world of entrepreneurship, solid business skills are essential. What are the general, as well as the specific, skills you might need for the business you choose? Are you considering a business that will use most of your present abilities, or will you need some training or education before you can start the business?

First, do your research. Make sure you know what specific skills and personality traits will be required for the particular business or industry you are considering. Which of your communication skills will you need to use the most? Will you be communicating mostly with the public or with your own staff? Do you shine when you're around strangers, or are you most comfortable with familiar faces? All the business skills in the world won't make a difference if you're an introvert trying to force yourself into a role that requires the personality traits of an extrovert ... or if you have math anxiety and hope to run a financial services firm!

Accounting and Finance Skills

Learning to read and interpret financial data is imperative to understanding your small business. Are you financially literate? Can you read a balance sheet or financial statement? We don't mean just reciting the sums at the bottom of a balance sheet or presuming that the net profit or loss amount at the bottom of a Profit & Loss (P&L) statement is an accurate reflection of the "bottom line." We mean fully understanding what these elements actually mean, what they are based on, and what they predict about the future.

In reality, unless someone is an accountant, banker, broker, or successful business owner with strong accounting skills, the average person cannot truly understand financial statements, and some good training is probably advisable. We recommend taking "Finance and Accounting for the Non-Financial Executive" or a similarly titled course through your community college or online programs.

Even if you recognize that finances are not your forte and your intent is to hire professionals to manage your accounting, you have to be able to understand if they are doing a good job for you. The sad reality is that many business owners discover that their financial "experts" aren't really experts at all, but it's already too late to undo the damage done by ignorant or unscrupulous hires. (See Chapter 9 for more on acquiring a trustworthy accountant.)

Administrative Skills

Many people who have never worked as an administrator hesitate to pursue their dreams of business ownership because they fear they have little or no administrative skills. However, many of these skills are transferable, common life skills. The abilities to plan, implement, prioritize tasks, schedule, manage projects and people, delegate, motivate, budget, and make decisions are administrative skills most people use in their daily lives. Just ask any multitasking parent!

Access your administrative skills by thinking of examples of times you have exercised them. Balancing a checkbook, planning a party or a remodeling project, coaching a team, creating a budget, supervising children, job hunting, attending school, and making good decisions are all tasks that utilize administrative skills required in every business.

Administrative abilities go beyond "hard" skills such as good organization. Effective administration also requires "soft" skills related to ethics, character, and personality. Your ability to listen, be creative, use appropriate social skills, have patience, show empathy, and inspire others are all valuable attributes for the business owner.

Management Skills

A good business manager can be compared to the conductor of an orchestra. The conductor must be aware of and knowledgeable about the many separate components that make up the orchestra and then bring them all together in a coordinated effort to produce one harmonious product. In the case of business management, those elements can include tangibles and intangibles, such as employee supervision, coordination of projects, assessment of output and input, budget creation and supervision, deployment of resources (human and material), and workplace morale and motivation.

Business management relies on many other skills covered in this section, such as good organizational and leadership abilities. Effective managers need expertise that includes defining plans of action and then providing guidance to follow those plans.

Before a plan of action can be created, tasks need to be broken down and assessed realistically. This involves more steps than most people realize. Assessing tasks includes the following activities:

- Scheduling when a task will be done.

- Allotting the proper time to complete it. This is actually one of the most difficult parts of task assessment. It requires an accurate, realistic sense of time as well as a thorough knowledge of the multiple aspects of the task.

- Setting deadlines for completion.

- Being aware of the effects of a task's completion and consequences of its incompletion.

- Determining what tools and supplies might be required.

- Estimating any costs.

- Delegating the task or portions of the task.

- Establishing who will perform the task.

- Prioritizing the importance of the task.

- Setting up tracking/supervisory systems to ensure the task is completed.

Management also includes making multiple decisions, which we cover next.

Decision-Making Skills

"To choose, it is first necessary to know."
—Herman Finer, Political Scientist

Near the heart of good management is the making of good decisions. Gaining confidence in decision making comes from gathering information, becoming knowledgeable, developing decision-making skills, accepting responsibility for decisions, and establishing a track record of successful results from decisions made. In addition, the ability to see one's decisions and outcomes as a learning process instead of a win-or-lose proposition helps build confidence.

Remember: The failure to make a decision is, by default, a decision ... and you may be surprised and disappointed by the outcome of your non-decision!

Leadership Skills

Entrepreneurship requires leadership skills. Motivational, inspirational, disciplinary, and role model skills will all be needed if you expect to manage people as well as your business. When it comes right down to it, can the two ever really be separated?

As a business owner, you will be ultimately responsible for all the persuading, encouraging, hiring, firing, disciplining, and evaluating of the people working for you. When your own money is at stake, acting decisively on employee issues is critical to your business.

Managing people is often classified as the toughest job there is in small business ownership. Because you will probably not be able to afford the insulation of layers of management between you and employees—and, to a degree, customers, contractors, and vendors—you will be in the direct line of fire. Leadership skills, however, go beyond managing others; they include managing yourself. True leaders are intimately aware of their strengths and weaknesses, their integrity and personal code of ethics, the effects all their actions (or inactions) have on others and their business, and their influential roles as educators and mentors.

Successful leaders know when to take command and when to let others take the lead. They choose their battles wisely, work on improving their mental and emotional strengths, and continually strive to improve themselves and others within their sphere of influence.

Don't forget: True leaders should never have to command respect. Instead, they earn it.

Marketing Skills

Few businesses can survive without marketing, advertising, and public relations. Developing a marketing plan and a realistic marketing budget will be vital to your success. While you do not need to be an expert in every type of market, you must understand what marketing and advertising methods will work best for your particular product or service. Marketing includes many skills, some of which can be outsourced, if you have the budget for it. If you don't, then prepare to develop your own marketing skills.

In today's competitive and tech-savvy business world, you will need to be knowledgeable about or have a plan for the following:

- Internet marketing, including how search engines like Google or social media sites like Facebook play a role in promoting a company.

- Building effective websites and creating Web-based marketing campaigns.

- Analyzing the results of various marketing campaigns and the return on investment (ROI) for each.

- Computer and software programs to enable the creation of simple brochures, newsletters, and ads.

- Graphic design, or an understanding of how colors and graphics are used in advertising and on websites. (The actual production of graphics can be outsourced.)

- Your market niche: who the people are you're trying to reach, their demographics, how to best reach them, and how to motivate them and convert them into customers.

- Direct-mail materials, e-mail promotional campaigns, and advertising opportunities.

- The writing of news releases or blogs and the best ways to distribute them.

Fortunately, many basic marketing skills can be acquired through classes at community colleges or via online courses or instructional CDs and DVDs. And there are many websites (such as www.elance.com) where you can find professional help at a reduced rate. Lastly, don't forget to take advantage of free publicity and public relations by participating in community, industry, and networking events.

Human Resource Skills

If you will be hiring employees, then you'll need the skills to recruit, interview, qualify, and fairly compensate them. Through our own hiring experiences, we've discovered that if you "hire smart," employees are an investment, not an expense. Always hire for skills and, to the extent possible, hire for values and work ethic.

Once you have identified the skills and related experience required, select people with positive attitudes. You can teach employees most of what you know, but rarely can you change their attitudes. We've found that, in general, people who are happy, optimistic, enthusiastic, and smiling will learn faster and be more flexible than unhappy ones. A great bonus is that optimistic employees will create great experiences for your customers.

While many businesses start out with no employees, your hope should be that your venture will grow so big that you will need assistance to handle all your customers. If you know you're going to need employees from the start, you'll want to have them hired and ready to go as close as possible to the anticipated "launch time" of your business.

Of course, hiring the best employees is only the start. Once they're on board, you'll either need to hire a human resources manager or you'll need to learn about employment regulations (state and federal), benefits and compensation best practices, tax categories, payroll coordination, company employment policies, and matters related to other HR responsibilities. Keep in mind that great *internal* customer service—treating employees well—will have a positive effect on external customer service.

Employees can be your greatest asset or your most damaging liability. Learning the proper (and legal) ways to hire and manage employees can save you time and money—and perhaps your business. In today's litigious society and with all the changing laws, many small businesses outsource their HR function to avoid or mitigate their risk and reduce cost. There are many companies that can provide these important services to you and your staff.

Customer Relations Skills

No business can survive without customers, so it follows that, in order to succeed, entrepreneurs should develop outstanding customer service skills. In fact, customer service is the "weapon" a small business can use to take business away from major competitors.

Whether you will have direct contact with customers or will be in charge of other people who do, your attitude, behavior, and example will influence the character of your business and how your customers are treated. Keep in mind this general rule of thumb: *The cost to obtain a new customer is as much as six times the amount needed to keep an existing one.*

In a small business, you are often the main contact your customers have with your company. Imprint your style and expectations into the culture of the company. Great internal customer service often transfers into great external customer service. You are literally "the face" of your business, so make it a friendly one! Keep these observations in mind:

- Every customer should feel his or her needs have been met after each experience with your company.

- Do not view customers as interruptions to your business but as opportunities to serve.

- See customer service as a skill to be continually supported and developed. Hone your skills and create a motivating environment for yourself and your employees that will help optimism grow.

- Learn to think from the perspective of your customers' interests. Make them feel valuable and appreciated. Whenever appropriate and possible, establish a personal rapport with them.

- Under-promise and over-deliver.

- See customer complaints as opportunities, a chance to sharpen your skills by satisfying them and possibly learning from them. For every customer who complains, there are usually several others who are also unhappy but simply choose to go elsewhere the next time they need a similar service or product.

- Let disgruntled customers vent their frustrations before you attempt to resolve their issue. Then go into action with alternative solutions.

- Be ready to accept responsibility for the results of your decisions and actions. The other—and shinier—side of this coin is the reward of knowing you made the right decision, accomplished a goal, or even made just one grumpy customer happy.

A good place to begin in developing your customer service skills is by adopting the Golden Rule and treating people like you would want to be treated in their situation. Put yourself in your customers' shoes and teach your employees to do the same. This principle in action creates a positive energy—a chain reaction, if you will—that affects all of those around you, even long after they've left your establishment.

If you want to actually *improve* on the Golden Rule, ask your customers about what *they* want and how they like to be treated—not just the way *you* would want to be treated in their place. You can't presume you know what all people want or how they like to do business. You must discover their unique needs, individual personalities, and the way they prefer to interact with a business owner or employees. Unless you're a mind reader, the best way to know your customers is by taking surveys, asking questions, and learning how each customer *really* feels.

 From the Desk of David Nilssen

My friend Sharon tells the story about a wonderful little restaurant that lost her business by being too friendly (which is rather ironic, since she can talk the ear off of strangers and brass statues alike!). Sharon and her husband used to frequent a local café with outstanding food. On a particularly slow day, they introduced themselves to the owner to compliment him on his business. Rather than expressing thanks and moving on, he sat down at their table and proceeded to chat with them throughout their meal. The next time the couple came in, the owner made a beeline for their table and joined them again. While they appreciated his friendly manner and the personal attention, they wanted to socialize with each other, not with him, and the situation became extremely uncomfortable. After this happened a third time, they decided to order their food "to go." Unfortunately, whenever the owner spied them, he'd run over and talk to them nonstop until they could grab their food and make a dash for the exit! Things finally became so awkward, they chose never to return.

In this case, the owner was practicing what he considered the Golden Rule: He obviously enjoyed talking and getting a lot of personal attention himself, so he presumed others would too. But his attempts to "do unto others as he would have others do unto him" only resulted in the loss of two customers. This is why it's so important to understand that, because every person is unique, you must determine what each of your customers actually wants and needs—not what you want and need!

The Importance of Self-Knowledge

As human beings, we can be categorized in various ways, including by our personality type. A number of popular "personality assessments" suggest, for example, that we are, by nature, leaders, followers, analysts, or influencers. The science of trying to understand our personal style has been around since Socrates, and assessments like DiSC®, Myers-Briggs, and others are designed to identify one's "core" style.

Any of the styles are applicable to a business, but matching your particular gifts to those required for success in a certain kind of business can make the difference between success and failure, between enthusiasm and hating to get up in the morning. For example, if you are analytical and low on social interaction skills, a business that requires a lot of cold calling may not be the best fit. Of course, you can buy the services of a sales rep, but often in the early stages of business development, you may need to strap on the selling shoes. From another perspective, if you are an impassioned leader and used to giving directives, how will you fare when you don't have delegates to delegate to? Will you need to hire the detail-oriented people sooner rather than later to make sure the business does not overlook critical operational details?

A note of clarification is warranted here as well. Being "hard-wired" to one style or another does not mean we do not have the ability to adapt. In fact, great leaders adapt to others' styles with seemingly little effort. Knowing your core style, however, is important, because you will perform best when concentrating your energy within the comfortable boundaries of your personal style. That's why we suggest, in the next section of this chapter, that you take a few different assessments, such as the DiSC® analysis and the StrengthsFinder®. These are designed to increase your level of insight regarding how you communicate, your best work environment, and your entrepreneurial aptitudes. They can help you find the right fit—and perhaps disqualify you from buying a particular kind of business.

Once you have a foundational understanding of your style and entrepreneurial adaptability, check your ego at the door. Keep an open mind in your quest for self-knowledge. In addition to taking assessments, get objective feedback from people you trust. Look at the reviews you had while employed and be honest with yourself. What are your gifts and where can you demonstrate competencies? And note, too, that the culture of a large organization can mask the potentially serious implications of mismatching your personality style and strengths with the mission-critical work that needs to be done in a small-company environment.

When the ancient Greeks coined the phrase "know thyself," they were on to something. Each of us has gifts and strengths than can be mobilized to constructive purpose, by simply acknowledging and leveraging those qualities.

Entrepreneur Exercises

What are your strengths and gifts? Have you learned anything from past reviews in your corporate life? What kind of business would allow you to spend a significant amount of time doing those things that enable you to make the greatest impact? Take a few moments to write down what you believe to be your greatest strengths. (Now is as good a time as any; the book will be here when you return.)

To take a more structured and guided approach to analyzing your attributes, consider completing some assessments that provide helpful information directly related to your potential success as an entrepreneur. There are many such assessments available. The ones we describe here are the StrengthsFinder® test, the SWOT Analysis, and the DiSC® assessment.

StrengthsFinder®

An assessment that can help you snap a candid picture of your skills, talents, and personality is the StrengthsFinder® test (www.strengthsfinder.com). This assessment was introduced in 2001 in the book *Now Discover Your Strengths*, by Marcus Buckingham and Donald O. Clifton. The book does a phenomenal job of showing people how they can nurture and grow their talents, and the assessment provides great feedback. You may discover that you actually have more business skills than you thought you did. Or you could find that your business acumen and personality strengths are a better match for a different role than the one you were hoping to play.

SWOT Analysis

Another excellent tool for exploring your abilities, as well as the viability of a business or project, is a SWOT Analysis. SWOT is an acronym based on Strengths, Weaknesses, Opportunities, and Threats. By analyzing these four characteristics in relation to yourself and to the business you're considering, you will better understand how to thrive as an entrepreneur. You might discover there is tremendous change coming to your industry. It's possible you'll find there is already an established competitor you feel inadequate to compete against. Or a SWOT Analysis could identify a unique process for delivering your product or service. It's even possible that going through the process will cause a new idea to spring to mind, making the prospects for success even better.

Use this simple matrix to begin performing a SWOT analysis:

STRENGTHS	WEAKNESSES
Strengths	Weakness
Strengths	Weakness
Strengths	Weakness
OPPORTUNITIES	**THREATS**
Opportunity	Threat
Opportunity	Threat
Opportunity	Threat

The SWOT is a starting point for evaluation—but it can also oversimplify the process. Use this exercise to evaluate where you need additional information.

Evaluating your SWOT will help you to build on your strengths, resolve your weaknesses, exploit opportunities, and avoid threats—all elements necessary for creating a strategic plan for your business—and for yourself.

The DiSC® Personality Report

Based on the work of psychologist William Moulton Marston, the DiSC® profiles four primary behavioral styles (Dominance, Influence, Steadiness, Conscientiousness), each with very distinct and predictable patterns of behavior. Understanding the DiSC® patterns has empowered thousands of business owners to better understand themselves and others. The results of the profile report are designed to provide targeted insights and strategies for interpersonal success through more effective communication, understanding, and tolerance. The DiSC® assessment can be used for personal growth and development, training, coaching, and management of individuals, groups, teams, and organizations.

The Online DiSC Profile (http://www.discprofile.com/) is used as a learning tool to create rapid rapport and connection with people and is considered by some to be a fundamental aid in sales, management, and leadership. The underlying rationale is that understanding behavioral styles benefits personal and professional relationships by improving communication skills and reducing conflict. The goal is to better understand what motivates people and to be able to recognize how to effectively deal with others.

From the Desk of David Nilssen

Each of us is wired differently, and we all possess unique talents—often very different than what we would expect. StrengthsFinder, in combination with a DiSC® assessment, helped me understand my unique talents and how to best use them in the workplace. Strengths-Finder was also a tremendous resource for my business partner, and our results helped us to identify where we would focus our time working in and on the business. My top five strengths are the following:

1. Activator—"Where can we start?" Activators are impatient for action. While they will concede that analysis has its place and discussion can sometimes provide valuable insights, deep down they know that only action is "real." Only action leads to performance, and once a decision is made, you cannot NOT act. Activators fit best into positions that allow them to be measured on outcome rather than process. Their process is not always pretty. They are particularly good with business start-ups or turnaround situations.

2. *Woo—Wooers see a roomful of strangers as friends they have not met and love the challenge of making people like them. They are quick to build rapport because they learn people's names, ask them questions, and strike up a conversation by focusing on common interests. They derive satisfaction out of making a connection; but once it is made, they are quick to wrap it up and move on. Wooers are great in jobs where they are interacting with lots of people. Elected office, business development, and outside sales are positions that require "woo."*

3. *Maximizer—Maximizers see potential everywhere, and they believe "excellence" is their measure. Taking something from below average to slightly above is not rewarding. Transforming something strong into something superb is much more thrilling. They like to polish the pearl until it shines. Maximizers should seek roles that allow them to coach, mentor, or teach.*

4. *Communicator—Communicators like to describe, host, speak in public, and write. Ideas are dry beginnings and events are static. They feel a need to bring them to life, to energize them, to make them exciting and vivid. They take the dry idea and enliven it with images, examples, and metaphors. As a result, people like to listen to them. Communicators will always do well in roles where they are paid to capture people's attention. Their strengths will probably flourish in teaching, sales, marketing, ministry, and media.*

5. *Competitor—When Competitors look at the world, they are instinctively aware of other people's*

*performance. Others' performance is their ultimate
yardstick. No matter how hard they tried, no matter
how worthy their intentions, if Competitors reach
their goal but do not outperform their peers, the
achievement feels hollow. Competitive individuals
should select work environments in which they
can measure their achievements against other
competitive individuals.*

*Interestingly enough, I was spending very little time
utilizing my strengths and was instead allowing
myself to get mired in all the details that suck the
energy out of me. This realization led me to change
my role to eliminate the work that bogged me down
and helped me focus on the things that would allow
me to have the greatest impact on the business and
in turn, it has brought me great enjoyment.*

Most people haven't taken a full inventory of their skills or
assessed their strengths. You probably have far more skills than you
realize. Taking stock of your abilities is an exercise that can inspire
the confidence you need to become an effective entrepreneur.

Patience as a Profitable Virtue: Stephen's Story

Every entrepreneur who starts a small business needs to be
patient while the business grows. Stephen redefined patience,
waiting four years before he could finally take his first paycheck.

His story begins when he joined with partners to start a small
business providing home blueprints on CD-ROMs. The company was moderately successful, but Stephen felt they needed
a different sales platform, and he made plans to convert to an
Internet-based business. He bought out the partners, took the
business online, and over time expanded to offer 16,000 home
plans from several hundred different designers and architects.

"After we built the website, sales slowly grew, but I eventually decided I needed to draw a line in the sand," Stephen says. "I picked a date and said that if the company didn't 'happen' by then, I would go back and get a real job."

As luck would have it, the "deadline month" was also the month the business took off. The company had previously averaged 20 plan sales per month, and Stephen hoped to increase sales to 40 plans per month. "When I drew the line at 40 plans," he says, "that month we sold 65 plans, and I knew I could take a check. It felt good, but the paycheck probably felt better to my wife; she had stood solidly behind me from the beginning."

Early on, the small business entered into a deal with Microsoft to get on their home page; the resulting traffic—largely untargeted—overwhelmed their servers. Stephen started focusing on Google advertising to find targeted leads, developing sophisticated keyword tools and analysis models. In time, ad spending grew to $120,000 per month.

"We ran it all through my American Express card," Stephen says, "and we were such good customers that at one point they offered me a black American Express card."

Even with sales exploding, the business stayed lean. At its peak Stephen took in $5 million in annual revenues with just five other employees: one in IT, three in customer service, and one in sales. The nature of the business made it completely virtual; in fact, when a customer placed an order, it was sent to partner designers and architects to fulfill. In effect, the company had no inventory—and no inventory costs.

"When I look back at what we were selling," Stephen says, "it was one of the perfect products for the Internet. For example, I would be afraid of buying a diamond over the Internet ... but buying a home plan is different. You see what the home looks like, you see the floor plans ... you don't need to physically touch it to recognize its value."

He also seized other opportunities to leverage success. Realizing a customer buying home plans was also in the market to spend hundreds of thousands of dollars on building materials, Stephen sold advertising space to manufacturers and distributors. "Talk about targeted," he says. "If you couldn't sell advertising on a site like ours, you couldn't sell advertising anywhere."

In fact, the small business became so successful that Stephen sold the company to another blueprint publisher.

Business skills are critical, as is tenacity and drive. Even in an Internet business, issues like whether servers are up and credit card processing is online are a constant concern.

"I also feel," he continues, "that if you're not self-motivated, you shouldn't run your own business. Running your own small business is harder than working at a corporate job."

Stephen believes his most important achievement is to have repaid his family's faith in his abilities.

3

Mentors

The dictionary defines a mentor as "a wise and trusted counselor or teacher; an influential senior sponsor or supporter." Mentors can be particularly helpful when you are in major times of transition in your life, and you may have already experienced the benefits of having a mentor—for example, when you entered college and were choosing a major, or when you were comparing job offers. Early in your career, perhaps a mentor helped you understand how to navigate a corporate culture.

Mentors differ from advisors and consultants, yet there is some overlap when wisdom and experience are shared. The main difference is that a mentor has an emotional connection to the welfare of the mentee. Mentors often are not paid, whereas advisors and consultants are rewarded with monetary compensation.

In the entrepreneur's world, which is often characterized by a strong sense of self-reliance and individualism, mentors can have a particularly powerful impact. They become part of the entrepreneur's support network.

In addition to your life experiences and perhaps the influence of a teacher in an educational setting, mentors can be among the most important factors in determining how your entrepreneurial career develops. They can inspire you and enhance your ability to see beyond your own limitations, thereby helping you to develop the confidence you may need to launch your enterprise and to persist through the challenges. They can offer an objective perspective when you're uncertain about which direction to take. And they can suggest alternatives that you may not have thought of on your own when you're dealing with unexpected circumstances or ongoing concerns.

Given their potential to play a major role in your success as an entrepreneur, mentors should be actively sought out. What should you look for in a mentor? Obviously, personal qualities are as important as professional expertise. A mentor should be someone you both like and respect. Ideal mentors are the kinds of people who are comfortable in their own success and who enjoy helping others. Look for mentors who are not in a business that competes with what you are doing but who have related experience in the same field and have ample wisdom to share.

Realistic expectations should be set within a mentor-mentee relationship. These individuals are not paid for their time and are not consultants hired to tell you what to do or how specifically to do it. That said, don't be afraid to ask a mentor for help. Mentors draw on their vast experience and expertise, and they listen and suggest, much as a coach would. A good mentor should help you come to your own conclusions. As an entrepreneur, *you* will be responsible for living with the results.

Two books we recommend are *Never Eat Alone* and *Who's Got Your Back*, both by Keith Ferrazzi, an expert on professional relationships. They contain additional information that will help you to develop support structures and mentor relationships.

From the Desk of Jeff Levy

I have had several mentors in my life who formed and influenced my entrepreneurial way of looking at the world. I think of them often and try to return the favor to future generations of entrepreneurs.

Don Mann became my first mentor when I was an undergraduate at Fordham University. Out of financial necessity I had to work full time and still get a solid education within my goal of four years. Don was the VP of marketing for a manufacturer's representative organization located in New York City. They would hire motivated students from Fordham, and I was employed to provide some general office help.

Don gave me the nastiest assignment one could think of—cleaning and organizing a storeroom that looked like a tsunami had gone through it, followed by a dirt storm, twice. After two days, I was ready to quit. I wasn't paying private school rates to spend my afternoons in storeroom hell, I told myself.

Don knew that it was a tough job. He was testing me for work ethic and organizational skills. After a few weeks he started to give me more assignments, equally challenging but requiring more thought and not as much sweat.

One day Don asked me, "Did you ever consider a business career?" This simple question from a respected mentor was profound. In my senior year I switched to night school, worked full time, and was offered a job in customer service. This was a new land of possibilities. Don eventually went on to form his own company, Pro-Med, and I am forever thankful that he took interest in me and took the time to ask me a simple but life-changing question.

My second mentor, Loren Manera, came into my life at a time when I had seized the opportunity to test my abilities and commitment to succeed. I volunteered for a very challenging assignment—selling a new-technology defibrillator, developed by Physio-Control in Redmond, Washington, to New York City hospitals. At the time, New York City ranked dead last out of 50 territories, and it had occupied that position for years.

The first thing Loren taught me was that if a door said "No Solicitors" and "Authorized Visitors Only," it was still OK to persist because I was there to help save lives, not sell; and he personally authorized me to go in. Talk about thinking out of the box creatively! I learned from this mentor that if you are doing good things, nothing can stand in your way. He taught me to "act with intent," a phrase that I often use today when coaching entrepreneurs to be successful. After one year, New York City was in the top 10 percent in the nation for number of defibrillator units placed in hospitals and emergency medical centers. We saved countless lives. I learned that I could make a difference and overcome a huge challenge for the right purpose.

My third mentor came along just after my first (and only) business failure. Bill Greenwood was a local investor in Washington State. I had moved to Seattle to work on an emerging company's new team, and I pitched him on investing in an idea. Bill invested and lost what, at that time, was a considerable amount of money.

Nevertheless, Bill saw some redeeming qualities in me and asked me to join his new company, Windswept Capital, as a partner. His vision was to invest in Seattle-based companies and provide them with management oversight. This mentor taught me that great things can come from failure and enormous challenges. You just don't give up on your dreams. In fact, you learn more from the hard times than you do when you happen to be in business during a boom economy. At Windswept, I was now an entrepreneur on a mission. One of our companies was acquired by a public company for a great return to us and our shareholders.

Tom Cross was my fourth mentor. He was the CFO of the publicly held company we worked for, and I knew he was a smart guy. After working together for five years, we developed a friendship. Tom was entrepreneurial and creative. We crafted a proposal and pulled together a team of investors and trusted managers to take three divisions from the public company and make them private, with ourselves being major shareholders. What I learned from Tom was that if the idea is sound, any obstacle, no matter what it is, can be overcome.

We raised the unbelievable sum of $35 million, had our offer accepted, and within 30 days took over the reins of a $65 million manufacturing company with about three hundred people operating in most of the developed countries of the world.

In recap, my mentors taught me that entrepreneur-
ship means these things:

- *Hard work—the willingness to do whatever is*
  necessary—is essential.
- *Talent can be overrated; perspiration still accounts*
  for 98 percent of success.
- *You don't win every time, but you never give up.*
- *Every problem has a solution.*
- *Dream big.*

After a very astute observation from my wife, I started
my own venture helping aspiring entrepreneurs to go
into business. I knew it was time to become a mentor
myself. Her advice was simple: You have had great
mentors; it is time to be one!

Who have your mentors been? You probably have already
had people fill this role in your life. Many people, some unknow-
ingly, teach us entrepreneurial lessons.

Seek out entrepreneurial mentors who impress you. When
possible, add them to your team as advisors—people you can
meet with every month or two to check your progress, and whom
you can call when needed. You do not have to go it alone. Build
a peer group, a team, and develop mentor relationships.

Tapping into Your Motivation

"The living self has one purpose only: to come into its own fullness of being."

—D. H. Lawrence

In this chapter we take a closer look at a topic that we've touched on before: motivation. To some extent this is a broad philosophical concept, but when you consider it on an individual level, you'll see that it is a foundational piece in understanding where you're coming from and where you want to go as an entrepreneur.

Because in many respects you are what you *do*, your characteristics, strengths, and weaknesses can be revealed by how you behave in your business. Behavior, in turn, can be affected to a major degree by the strength of your conviction and motivation. Positive motivation is likely to bring out the best in you, whereas negative motivation—or a complete lack of motivation—will likely result in less than optimal performance in whatever you choose to do.

Defining Your Motivation

There's no question that motivation is an integral component of entrepreneurship. In fact, we would argue that motivation is the deciding factor in what separates those who successfully make the transition to self-employment and self-reliance. If you are not motivated, then the normal "stuff" the world throws at people who try to be different will beat you down.

It's important to define and understand what motivates you to action, and then to follow through and develop that motivating element. An employee who dreams of becoming an entrepreneur, browses the Internet looking for businesses for sale, but never acts is most likely not adequately motivated. You need motivation—followed by action—to start, buy, or operate a successful business.

Many businesses fail within the first year. Some of these fail only because the entrepreneur ran into an unforeseen event and did not have the ongoing positive motivation to do whatever it took to keep going. Giving up and closing the doors may have seemed like the only option, perhaps as an excuse to run for cover under the perceived security umbrella of employment.

As we've pointed out before, many employees might hate their jobs or their boss and dream of leaving, yet they get up day after day and report to work, never taking any steps toward becoming entrepreneurs. How does one create or find the motivation to make the transition from employee to employer?

Some people who dream of becoming entrepreneurs might initially be motivated by money. But be forewarned: money is a thin motivator. It is one result of your hard work and your pursuit of your passion. Working for money alone won't necessarily sustain you when the going gets tough.

On the other hand, money linked to a larger purpose can provide the kind of motivation that endures. Consider these examples of positive motivation:

- I want to have a lifestyle that enables me to spend as much time as possible with my family and to create financial security for them.

- I want the independence to set my own schedule, to determine my own time of retirement, and to have the financial freedom to pursue my non-work-related interests and hobbies.

- I want to accumulate enough wealth to make a significant, perpetual contribution to my favorite charitable organization.

One of the benefits of entrepreneurship is the power of choice. You have the ability to make money in proportion to your efforts, and you have the choice to satisfy your *true* motivation, be that family, travel, time to spend as you wish, or philanthropy. Many of you know the story of TOMS Shoes. But for those who don't, here's how it's described on the company website:

> In 2006, American traveler Blake Mycoskie befriended children in Argentina and found they had no shoes to protect their feet. Wanting to help, he created TOMS Shoes, a company that would match every pair of shoes purchased with a pair of new shoes given to a child in need. One for One. Blake returned to Argentina with a group of family, friends and staff later that year with 10,000 pairs of shoes made possible by TOMS customers.

We can't imagine a more intriguing and inspiring example of positive entrepreneurial motivation!

When you start a venture, it is full of challenges and obstacles. (As we've said before, if it were easy, we would have a lot more entrepreneurs.) Where does one get the motivation to overcome the difficulties and achieve something? It comes from creating a vision and committing every resource at your disposal to pursuing it. It comes from passion—not passion about a product, hobby, or market, but a true emotional connection that relates to the most important thing you possess: your time on this earth and what you want to do with it. That is the ultimate source of motivation.

As this discussion makes clear, goals are an important component of motivation. To a large extent, motivation is all about defining your life goals and determining achievable benchmarks so you can reach for something that has a profound, positive impact on your life.

Once you've defined your broad life goals, you also need to establish concrete, practical goals, including monetary goals. Monetary goals must include your expectations for what it will cost to run the business and a good understanding of what it costs to run your household. If this business is to support you and your family, it has to cover its expenses and generate enough positive cash flow to meet your personal needs. And personal needs must include both current and future expenses, including retirement planning.

> *"No Goals, No Glory"*
> —Motto of the US Olympic Hockey Team

 From the Desk of David Nilssen

I recently had an experience that illustrates how motivation can sometimes be triggered by accidental occurrences. In our business, we do "brown bag" learning lunches. This particular day, my business partner was running a "goal-setting" meeting because it was January of 2010; we felt a conversation on the topic of setting goals was timely. Much of the time was spent on "finding your real motivation." We know that most people set New Year's resolutions but fail to meet them. Our belief is that those goals are never achieved because while the "what" is clear, the "why" is not.

During the meeting, one of our employees bravely shared his experience of what it was like growing up without his mother, who had died when he was just a child. He expressed how difficult that was and how much he wished she could have been alive to meet her grandchildren. This intimate confession brought the entire room to tears.

His vulnerability inadvertently struck a nerve with another person in the room, whom I will refer to as "Tom." Tom had struggled significantly with his weight. At five foot four, he tipped the scales at 285 pounds. Listening to our mutual friend triggered a powerful motivational impulse in Tom. The thought of not being around for his two boys and daughter and future grandchildren was the motive he needed to lose 100 pounds in one year! That day he made a commitment in front of our entire company that he would lose 100 pounds. For a year, he walked during lunchtime, worked out at the gym, changed his eating habits, and inspired our company—and his family—to be healthier.

On January 3, 2011, after celebrating the Christmas and New Year holiday, he weighed in at our All Company Meeting. Tom had lost two pounds more than his goal! It's a simple story, but it illustrates the point that if you find what truly motivates you, anything is possible.

Only when you have determined your most important life goals and have set the vision can you commit fully to the particular business you choose. *Working with intent* is an important concept in this regard. In purely practical terms, working with intent will likely reduce the time between start-up and making money, which is an important consideration. You must understand the key factors that will accelerate your success and work on them with laser focus and a high sense of urgency. Particularly in the early stages of developing your business, the only thing you control is your time. Use it wisely—*intent*ionally—because it is the most precious resource you own. Don't let untoward diversions steal your time.

From the Desk of Jeff Levy

An observation that I have made that has evolved into a coaching point is that running from something is not a sustainable motivation upon which to build a business. Many entrepreneurial dreamers have their initial visit with me or attend one of my seminars because they were laid off from the job; they are bitter and angry. Often they will say that their goal in life is never to be in a position again where they can be downsized, right-sized, off-shored, or just plain laid off. Although that might be an understandable starting point, if people stick with that as their main motivation, I try to encourage them to be more introspective and concentrate on where they are going, not where they have come from. When in a significant career transition, don't immediately think about what you want to do, but rather strive to answer the query, Who am I? I have followed this process, and it helped create the foundation for my own self-employment decisions.

Tapping into Motivation: Allyn and Michelle's Story

Both Allyn and Michelle have medical backgrounds. Allyn was an Army Corps nurse, and Michelle has a master's in nursing education and worked for nine years in a Medicare home care agency. For a long time Allyn wanted to own a business, and both of them wished to continue helping others while using their nursing skills. They were very happy to find a franchise-based home health care provider that serves all ages, but primarily the elderly. Clients receive excellent care from qualified nurses and care providers within their own homes.

"We broke even a long time ago, and we're just a little over a year old. We've grown through the recession. ... We have a very strong foundation, and we have a lot of good quality growth," says Allyn.

"All we had to do was follow the model that they have in place. They have it all very fine-tuned: the exact dollar, exact sale. There are 160 locations now nationwide, and we are number 32 in the nation [as of July 2008]. I know about 60 other owners throughout the country, and I talk to them all the time about how they grow their businesses, what works for them."

Allyn and Michelle have a strong team of 115 employees. The praise and positive feedback that they receive from families and clients is what keeps them motivated and excited about the work. "Whether it's someone who has had an injury like a hip fracture or a family dealing with someone with severe dementia, clients are giving us feedback about how much they appreciate our help."

Entrepreneur Flaws and Weaknesses

"A man must know his limitations."

—Clint Eastwood

Prosperous entrepreneurs operate from strength and develop their strong points to become masterful at using these skills. They also continually assess themselves and are aware of their weaknesses.

Some weaknesses can be overcome by other strengths, some can be improved, and some are fatal to the entrepreneur. In this chapter we take a look at some of the most common flaws and weaknesses, describe how they can affect your prospects for success, and point out ways to avoid or diminish them.

Assuming or Being Quick to Judge

Making assumptions without merit can be detrimental and a fatal flaw for an entrepreneur. Extending credit by presuming someone will pay you because the person seems to have money can cost you plenty. Being quick to judge others by their actions can also be costly. Assuming someone is incapable based on hearsay can lead you to dismiss a stellar employee.

Decisions should be based on information and instincts. Make sure you have all the facts available before making a decision.

The Battle of the Little Bighorn, also known as "Custer's Last Stand," was a tragic end for George Armstrong Custer and his men, all because Custer made assumptions, including the following:

- Custer assumed that his soldiers would be fighting only 800 Native Americans. He had heard that approximately that many had left the reservations to fight, and he based his assumption on that number without sending a scout to check. Estimates suggest that at the time of the battle, there were actually about 3,000 fighting alongside Sitting Bull.

- Custer also assumed that the tribesmen would be asleep when he attacked. They were not.

- Custer assumed his opponents would scatter and run when they saw his troops. As we know, they did not.

Assumptions can be fatal. Even small assumptions that lead to negative consequences can cause you to lose confidence in your decision-making ability and cause employees to lose trust.

Unclear Goals or Lack of Vision

A lack of vision or defined goals keeps the entrepreneur from success. Because entrepreneurs need many of the skills of leaders, and leaders need followers or employees, a leader without a clear path will often lose commitments from others or create a state of confusion. A strong statement of your vision inspires others and builds motivation.

Failure to Delegate

Often when entrepreneurs start businesses, they develop systems and procedures. As the business grows, so do the owner's responsibilities, and many of the tasks the owner once performed now need to be handed off to assistants and associates, or outsourced. Some entrepreneurs feel no one can do the job or specific task as well as they do—after all, successful completion of these kinds of tasks is what boosted them to their current status. The entrepreneur who makes this mistake might become a micromanager. Restricting employees from taking responsibility can cause them to become distrustful and to feel powerless, lowering morale. The entrepreneur's business can become stagnant, unable to grow because handling so many smaller tasks makes running the business cumbersome. Employees cannot grow by being denied responsibility. The entrepreneur with this weakness needs to recognize that although others might not be quite as good at a task as he or she is, or the employee might not perform the task in quite the same way, if the employee (or outsourcing process) can achieve satisfactory results, the means might not be so critical. A familiar saying to keep in mind in this situation is this: "Do not let the perfect get in the way of the good."

In order to grow, the entrepreneur will have to "let go." Set clear objectives for your staff and do regular check-ins. If you have to, you can "course correct" without the staff or team going too far off course. This approach will help you scale the impact you have, empower the team to grow, and allow you to stay connected to the progress.

Rigidness

An entrepreneur who is not open to new ideas or resists change can be demoralizing to others. Refusal to listen to others or entertain innovations is a trait that can cause a company to fall behind competitors.

Successful entrepreneurs seek advice and consider input from others. They see people as resources and know that even adversaries can offer opportunities for gaining information.

In fact, while others might find comfort in familiar processes or rules, an entrepreneur should be energized by change. Change is an opportunity for creativity, innovation, devising new options, closing new partnerships. Entrepreneurs must be flexible and embrace change.

Indecisiveness

Someone who is indecisive often suffers from fear, uncertainty, and doubt. As we discussed in Chapter 1, fear is caused by a lack of knowledge. Poor decision-making skills are hazardous for anyone, and more so for a business owner. Indecisiveness can lead to systemic problems within an organization. Most of the time employees will shy away from those who lack firmness and are unable to make a decision. Staff members who are entrepreneurially inclined will grow frustrated because their leaders hesitate, move slowly, and miss out on opportunities.

While the best entrepreneurs can make good decisions even with imperfect data, you're likely to find it helpful to take specific steps to help get rid of indecisiveness. First, replace your fear or ignorance with knowledge. Ask lots of questions, request more data, and then take action on the information you have received. Second, be clear about the outcome you want. If you know what you want, the data you gather should help inform a quick decision. Lastly, picture yourself as a decisive leader. Create a visual image and remind yourself that you are capable of making good decisions quickly. Shift the image you have of yourself so you can confidently make decisions that affect your business.

Poor Communication Skills

Education and experience are useless when good communication skills are absent. You need to be effective at casting a vision, motivating employees, and explaining the "why" behind projects.

Many new entrepreneurs struggle to communicate with their teams. Their mistakes may include the following:

- Lack of timely response to others
- Contacting people and stating only self-serving purposes

- Not following up
- Being dishonest
- Being disrespectful
- Neglecting formalities or courtesy
- Ignoring messages or not returning calls
- Complaining, blaming, or being negative
- Making assumptions
- Not providing enough background

Great communicators provide helpful context and deliver complete information—they tell the whole story. They deliver stories without too much repetition and are clear, concise, and use the proper voice inflection. In the book *The Power of Body Language*, author Tonya Reiman states that people watch how you deliver a message as much as they listen to the words you speak. Practice becoming an effective storyteller and mind your body language. Use gestures where appropriate—but don't overdo it. The ability to listen, interpret, express thoughts and ideas, and follow acceptable practices is vital to the successful entrepreneur.

6

Entrepreneur Development

Many motivational speakers, business coaches, and gurus present lists of skills and characteristics similar to what we've presented in this book. However, information about how to actually *develop* these qualities is scarce, and that's the focus of this chapter. Remember that developing yourself as an entrepreneur is not easy. Human nature tends to lead us to stay with the efforts that are most comfortable. Entrepreneur development, on the other hand, will stretch and challenge you. You may have been born with certain gifts, but they will need to be expanded by experience and ongoing education.

Many experts seem to think we can develop entrepreneurial characteristics by simply being made aware of them—as if a "positive attitude" or becoming "goal oriented" is something that can be instantly turned on. In fact, consistent self-development is a lifelong pursuit, and there are things you can do to improve the entrepreneurial traits you possess and to acquire the others that are necessary for success.

Become a Master Builder

A master builder begins with a thought or an idea. The thought goes from abstraction to creation through a physical relationship with the tools of choice: paint, canvas, brushes, clay, stone, and so on.

Likewise, the attributes of the entrepreneur—attitudes, virtues, skills, goals, and strategies—are abstract. Abstract thinking is good, but you need to create physical relationships with these attributes to develop them. To turn these abstracts into physical reality, use the tool of *action*. More specifically, take action in these three areas: (1) delineating your goals, (2) developing new habits, and (3) seeking out role models.

Goals.   Define and write down your goals for the day, the week, the month, and the year. Writing things down causes a psychological interaction between the physical act of writing and seeing what you have written, creating a feedback loop in your brain.

Set benchmarks for your goals so you can measure your progress. How much closer are you to owning a business than you were last week? Write down the simplest accomplishments that move you toward your goal, such as reading this book. If you measure your progress in small steps, you will still go a long way. A wise person once said, "A journey of a thousand miles starts with one step."

Assign a timetable for each of your goals. Without a deadline, your goals can drift along and remain unfulfilled for years. Set realistic deadlines and strive to meet them. Give yourself extensions when necessary. Reward yourself when goals are met.

Review your goals every day. Keep your list where you can see it throughout the day.

Habits. How can you transform your brain into the entrepreneurial brain? You can become a leader and an entrepreneur by changing your thoughts and adopting new habits that will change your beliefs and actions.

Make a list of the habits you would like to develop that are beneficial to becoming an entrepreneur. These could be things like reading about marketing trends or self-improvement 10 minutes each day, meeting with a mentor once a month, or setting aside time every Sunday to plan for the upcoming week.

Then start small by picking one or two daily tasks and practice these actions every day. If you practice an action for 21 days, it will become a habit. If you find that maintaining the action for 21 days was easy, then either increase the time you devote to the action or make the task a little more difficult.

If you cannot maintain any action for 21 days, try a less ambitious goal. The smaller the actions are, the less likely you are to circumvent them.

Role Models. Search for successful entrepreneurs who exemplify the attributes and habits you desire to develop. If possible, meet and talk with them, see them work, and note their examples. What you learn can help you model yourself as a successful entrepreneur.

Cultivate Balanced Optimism

Running a small business is stressful. To survive, you must have balanced optimism, which is one of the attributes we listed in Chapter 1.

Your thoughts affect all aspects of your life. It is possible that your internal voice is reinforcing negative thoughts that inappropriately manifest themselves in other parts of your life. Many people who pay attention to their thoughts come to realize that much of their thinking is negative. Letting go of these thoughts can be liberating, and it does not take significant effort.

Begin by simply picturing yourself as a successful entrepreneur. Think about how you will demonstrate your ability to lead. What will you do to show that you have the following attributes?

- Competitive
- Decisive
- Flexible
- Goal-oriented
- Good communicator
- Hard working
- Self-disciplined

Remember, to a certain extent, your thoughts become your reality. Avoid using negative words like "can't" or "should "or "never." Purge negative thoughts and words if at all possible. Allow yourself to see how successful you can be—and will be!

Develop Listening Skills

As noted in earlier chapters, good communication skills are essential for success as an entrepreneur. But many people think of communication only in terms of speaking. They forget the other side of the equation—namely, listening.

Practice listening to others and evaluating their information. Pay attention to their words, timing, voice inflection, and body language. By developing good listening skills, you can often determine a talker's emotional state, feelings or lack of feelings, honesty, sincerity, and objectives—and this can be critical to making good decisions, among other things.

Confirm that you have heard others when you respond, and confirm that you have been heard. Repeating your interpretation of what someone has just stated and asking that person for confirmation of your interpretation is one way of developing clear communication.

Make Personal Development a Priority

Don't wait until the end of the day to see if you have the time and energy to read something related to your personal development. Make your personal development a priority; schedule personal development appointments with yourself each week. Arrange a place where you will be uninterrupted. Make this place comfortable so you will look forward to this time alone. Use this time to read and do research. Make a list of reading material for the year. In addition, always keep a book handy for when you are traveling or waiting somewhere. Continuously increase your knowledge of your industry and the market.

✳ ✳ ✳

These suggestions don't require a major overhaul of your life, but they do require conscientious effort on your part. They represent the proactive approach that's essential if you want to move from dreaming about being an entrepreneur to actually becoming one.

Section II:
Your Business

7

Choosing a Business

Now that you are armed with self-knowledge and awareness, you can begin to narrow the target area. You have several options to consider: you can start a business (retail, service, manufacturing, Internet, consultant, and so on), buy an existing business, or seek a franchise award.

The difference between starting and buying a business is significant. In the former situation, you have to make every decision; in the latter you begin to run an organization that already has momentum, and so the choices you make are more long term. The decision to start your own business means making your own choices regarding such things as product, pricing, distribution, and promotion strategies. In general, this option is best suited for thoughtful entrepreneurs who have good planning skills. Acquiring an ongoing operation is best suited for those with a sound operational background. Franchise choice is somewhere in between the two—you are tasked with implementing a proven system that includes an already well-defined set of business tools. (We cover franchises in depth later in this chapter.)

Looking at Trends

Begin to narrow your search by talking with friends, family, and associates. What are they buying now, and what purchases are they considering in the near future?

Watch for emerging trends in business or society. Trends are not necessarily new products or new businesses. For example, newly reported health benefits of a product, such as the blood-pressure-lowering effect of hot tubs, could be announced, prompting an increase in sales. Always look for the unfulfilled need. Trends are created and affected by several factors, including the following:

- **News**—Product news, recalls, emerging technologies, and emerging markets are often reported in the popular press and in trade journals.

- **Discoveries**—Creative applications or new ways of doing things are the realm of entrepreneurship.

- **Government Regulations**—Opportunities are often created as government identifies issues and obstacles. An example is hands-free devices in automobiles.

- **Public Opinion or Demand**—This factor is always changing and evolving. Think of how Microsoft has positioned BING as a response to the unfocused methods of other search engines.

- **Demographic Changes**—Major shifts signal major opportunities. Have you thought about the emergence of retiring baby boomers as an economic force?

Who is likely to notice and respond to the trends you identify? These are your potential customers. There are likely to be many consumer subgroups categorized by age, gender, location, income, and other factors who might find this trend particularly attractive. Would you be good at working with and motivating a particular market segment? And—more important—is this trend likely to continue?

Another consideration for business ideas is to look at the problems and challenges that surround you in your own life. These can serve as inspiration for a problem-solving product or service. There's a reason why the expression "Necessity is the mother of invention" has been used so much it's now a cliché!

Once you have some ideas of what the market wants, you can assess the feasibility of a business model that would meet those market needs and then review your applicable skills.

Matching Your Skills

Naturally, your business opportunity will need to match your skills and interests and be financially feasible. Just because you discover a trend toward building and selling electric cars does not mean you will be able to obtain the funds to open an auto plant or dealership. However, you might have the expertise that lends itself to creating a specialized product or component *for* electric cars.

Review the relevant skills lists we presented earlier in this book. Select the skills that you think would be beneficial to the business you are considering. Then take a candid look at what you're naturally good at, what you really enjoy, and where you might happily apply your energies. For example,

- What are your hobbies or interests? Are you a good cook? Are you good with kids?

- What is your education specialization?

- What did you dream of being when you grew up?

- What skills have you learned in previous jobs that you're still using and enjoying today?

These considerations will help point you in the right direction. As the saying goes: *"If you work at what you love, you will love your work."*

Making a List

Put your ideas (no matter how on the edge they seem) down on paper. Make a list of five to seven possible niche markets that could support your idea, and then research each one. Here are some examples: software for emerging cloud-computing users; services for adults who need to care for aging parents; better integration of technology for in-home use; consulting services for small businesses; applications for smartphones and other devices. The list is endless, and you are limited only by your own creativity.

The United States Chamber of Commerce Small Business Center offers a Business Selection Checklist that can be used to help you narrow down your choices. The checklist is available for download at www.uschamber.com/sb.

Using the Business Selection Checklist, you will be able to rank the businesses you're considering by your interest in them and then rate each business within specific categories. You can rate them by your level of knowledge of the business, the experience and skills you possess that are relevant to the business, and the ease of entry and uniqueness of the business. You will find the US Chamber website to be packed with good ideas and information on helping you to choose a business.

Types of Businesses

Businesses, both franchise and non-franchise, come in several variations, and the differences often overlap one another. Here are the four basic types of businesses:

- **Product Sales**—In this business type, you buy and sell. You buy a product and sell it at a margin between what it costs you to purchase or manufacture and what the market will pay. You may hold inventory and be responsible for those carrying costs associated with storage, shipping, and other activities. Companies that sell products through the Internet—on e-Bay, Amazon.com, or the like—fit into this category.

- **Product Development**—In this business type, you develop products or help others develop products. Engineering, manufacturing, sourcing methods, overseas production, and patent knowledge are helpful skills.

- **Service**—Service businesses often require the least start-up costs. You do not need to buy and maintain inventory; you just advertise, staff properly, and perform services. Some businesses offer personal services (e.g., residential cleaning), and others are aimed at other businesses (e.g., document shredding). You might provide physical services, such as selling real estate, home remodeling, catering, custodial services, or delivery services. You might be considering virtual services, such as creating graphics, ghostwriting, or other intellectual offerings.

- **Restaurants**—This business type offers a significant outlet for creativity and also many structured approaches, such as franchise food operations. Food service does tend to require longer hours, including evenings and weekends. Trends can affect the long-term viability of the establishment.

Start-up or Buy a Business?

Why should someone consider buying a business versus starting one? What are the main differences between the two? Let's look at the differences. Here is how BING, the search engine from Microsoft, defines what an entrepreneur is:

entrepreneur—risk-taking business person; somebody who initiates or finances new commercial enterprises

Entrepreneurs initiate an enterprise. Small-business owners can be, and often are, individuals who buy a business from an entrepreneur. Buying a business is how many people enter business ownership. Like everything in life, buying a business or starting one has positive and negative sides.

For now, let's focus on buying a business. Two of the major benefits to buying an established business are simply reducing risk and having immediate access to income. Additionally, buying a business can come with immediate access to a working operation, customers, suppliers, inventory, and trained employees. Something that is often missed is the fact that when you buy someone's business, you are buying into owner's expertise. Usually the seller will train for a limited period of time. One thing the seller will not do, however, is teach basic business skills. The buyer has to have the skills and knowledge to run a business prior to purchasing one.

Buying an existing business can significantly reduce your risk, but it is not without its challenges. Employee and customer loyalty should be two major considerations. There are many individuals who acquire a business as an "absentee owner"—meaning they do not intend to work there. While this is certainly possible, we believe a business must be tended to like a garden. It needs constant attention. Otherwise bugs, weeds, and other issues can impair its growth. The best gardens are tended with love and constant attention.

In sum, acquiring an established business offers a quick jump into income-producing ownership. This approach also saves years of hard work and the uncertainty of start-ups.

Franchises

Franchises are perhaps the most misunderstood form of commercial enterprises. They are quite different from the "business opportunities" discussed on late-night TV or multilevel marketing options such as Amway® programs. This misperception is in part created by the fact that retail food franchises are omnipresent and all over the media. But franchises aren't just about fast food. Franchises can be in service areas, manufacturing, consulting, training, mentoring, or coaching; they can be business-to-consumer, business-to-business, work-from-home—the possibilities are numerous.

Franchises are an important option because most entrepreneur dreamers don't have all the skills necessary to take a business from infancy to maturity, and starting a business without the basic skills in place can be a recipe for failure. As we've discussed in previous chapters, developing a successful enterprise requires vision, as well as management, financial, marketing, sales, technical, and other skills—not to mention a unique idea and market position.

A franchise award can significantly close the gap between wanting to be in business and actually implementing a business plan. What has been said many times before but bears repeating is that in a franchise you are in business *for* yourself but not *by* yourself. You get the rewards and advantages of owning your own business, but you also get the power of being in a larger organization dedicated to one mission and goal. However, you do give up some profitability and control by a franchise award versus starting an independent, non-franchise model.

In a franchise, most of the unknowns are taken out of the equation. You begin with a recognized brand, logo, and uniformity of product offering. All the ancillary items like point-of-sale system, accounting software, brochure design, and physical layout are provided. In effect, you have three sturdy pillars on which to build a business: (1) brand name, (2) operating system, and (3) ongoing support and training. In addition, there are state and federally mandated reporting requirements that all franchise companies must follow to properly keep the prospective franchisee informed. By having the fundamental decisions already thought through, franchise owners can spend more time implementing and developing their business. Decisions are based on what has proven to work in the past, and a lot of the unknowns and their related risks are eliminated.

Franchises are not for everyone. If you cannot follow a set system and must do things your own way, avoid the franchise model.

Franchise systems create guardrails, rules, and other limits that are designed to keep you safe so you can proceed on your business-building journey. With those limitations, some degree of creativity is lost. However, rule number one in beginning a venture is always to increase your likelihood for success. While some may see franchise restrictions and rules as limiting creativity, many see following the franchise system as a way to limit the potential for failure.

Given all the franchise possibilities out there, how do you decide which one might be right for you? The first step in making a good choice (in addition to the points made earlier in this chapter) is to know what it is you are looking for in terms of a financial return, considering your ultimate financial goals and the realities of your starting point. Can you find similar examples of return on investment within the franchise system? And looking beyond the financial aspects of the business, what do the owners do each day? Is their lifestyle something that you want to emulate?

Without help, there is a significant chance that you may choose the wrong franchise. To avoid that possibility, you might consider working with a franchise coach. Franchise coaching services are in high demand because there are a limited number of franchise organizations—about 4,500—and an almost unlimited number of entrepreneurial dreamers. Often a person looking for franchise information gets overwhelmed by the clutter. The Internet is not necessarily the best source of information because it's poorly organized for getting specific and comprehensive data. That said, one website worth visiting for information on franchise coaching organizations is the website of the International Franchise Association (www.franchise.org).

Even if you work with a coach, it's important to be armed with facts in order to make good choices. As an informed client working with a franchise coach, you can more effectively determine what the experience would be like if you were awarded a specific franchise. Working with the information you initially provide, a coach can help you focus on your goals and help you sort through the options for a business that can help you to achieve your dream.

A franchise can be the key to your self-employment future with much less at risk than starting an independent venture. It's worth serious consideration.

Identifying Opportunities

"The main thing is to know and seize the critical moment."
—Cardinal de Retz

Timing is critical to business and the entrepreneur. But being in the right place at the right time is not enough. You must be *aware* that you are there, and you must have the tools and be prepared to take advantage of your position. And how do you become aware? You do so by obtaining relevant knowledge about current and near-future market needs and desires.

Determining what the market needs or wants at any particular time involves research. While it's wonderful if you can afford a market research professional or company to do this for you, you can do a lot of research on your own at no expense other than your time and energy.

Begin by reviewing the mainstream press: local and national websites, newspapers such as the *New York Times* and the *Wall Street Journal*, magazines like *Time* and *Newsweek*, and any specific industry publications that interest you. Review the business press, your local Chamber of Commerce publications, *Fortune, Forbes, Business Week,* and similar publications. Research websites on marketing and business trends, and read current blogs. There is a part of market timing that is counter-intuitive. Specifically, we see many businesses launching during recessions, when many would-be entrepreneurs stay on the sidelines waiting for the economy to strengthen. But waiting for a recovery may be too late. A down economy may actually be the right time to start a business for a variety of reasons: opportunities may open as competitors struggle; lower equipment pricing and interest rates are likely; labor costs may become more competitive; lease concessions may be available. Despite the difficulties of weathering a recession, it's important to keep in mind that history shows that we eventually return to growth.

At a recent large networking event, where nine new companies were recognized for starting up during 2009, one of the panelists was asked, "Is now a good time to start a business?" Her answer was this: "Entrepreneurs start businesses in both up and down economies; it doesn't matter. What they are looking for is the opportunity to meet a need."

Lenora Edwards is a business coach with the right attitude. She writes the following:

> There is something about humans that makes us feel more comfortable when we are following the herd. Perhaps it is the perception of safety in numbers. Maybe it is a carryover that if I am one in many, I won't get slaughtered. That might work for buffaloes, but not business men and women. Just look into the eyes of those who got layoff notices at Washington Mutual, Macy's, Microsoft, and I can go on and on. The herd provided little protection. Today's entrepreneurs do step out of the crowd in search of their dream and in pursuit of their goals.

There is no doubt that times of high unemployment stimulate new venture activity. Necessity remains the mother of invention. But as active entrepreneurs and businessmen for many years now, the two of us have come to believe that, while the pink slip may be the initial spark, it falls far short of providing the overall motivation for success. As we've said in previous chapters, it's not about running *from* something, but rather, it's about running *to* something—your future.

The Opportunity Is Now

When commerce is done in a bubble economy, all businesses tend to look good. Customers have discretionary income, market growth seems to be never-ending, and bad decisions seem to have less impact. When the economic world gets hit hard and business shrinks, as in the fourth quarter of 2008, companies with poor foundations begin to show cracks—sometimes fatal ones. While this can strike fear in the hearts of entrepreneurial dreamers (and everyone else!), it can also create great opportunities for visionaries who see windows opening. Perhaps they see that companies with a previously rock-solid hold on customers might be more vulnerable to new competitors who are better, faster, and offer more value. Or those companies may, in their efforts to survive, be open to considering new vendors or services without the blue-chip credentials of more established, high-end suppliers.

Over the years, we have seen markets open up to new companies when existing organizations fumbled and faltered during a change in economic environments. Recessions spawn special circumstances. While some watch the financial news looking for signs of economic hope, others are jotting down the business opportunities they see flashing amidst the gray clouds.

If interest rates are unusually low—or companies are drastically reducing inventory—could there be a better time to buy start-up equipment? What about the enlarged labor pool more open to work for your new company at more reasonable pay?

How often do you get a chance to negotiate a lease from a position of strength?

As we stated earlier, history proves that economies always come back. So is there a better time to position your new venture for the coming economic stabilization? If you are waiting for the *Wall Street Journal* or the Federal Reserve to declare a recession or economic downturn is over before you launch your business, it could very well be too late.

Coaching and Management Training as a Business: Chris's Story

A franchise award is not quite like buying a small business. When you buy a franchise, the system behind it has been tested repeatedly, and deviating from the proscribed system is not a recipe for success. This is not to say that franchisees can't take any creative control; but Chris, a franchisee of a management-training business, found that sometimes the best model truly is the one that others have established. This is particularly true when you are just beginning.

Chris had a background in education, first as a coach and teacher. When he entered the business world, he excelled in sales, which allowed him to move through the management ranks. Eventually he was combining his business expertise with his educational background by working as a trainer and business developer internationally.

"I realized as I was entering my 50s that jumping around from job to job isn't fun, especially in a tough economy," Chris says. "I felt like I didn't have control of my future. ... I looked around at different businesses. I toyed with consulting and realized that I wasn't the explorer; I was more of a farmer. And I wasn't someone who was going to come up with some new widget or new method or new technology. The idea of getting involved in a business that already existed, that already had the process in place, made sense."

Chris began looking at options with a franchise coach. During the coaching process he was able to eliminate many paths that didn't really match his skills. Management and leadership had been his strongest points for years, and this led him to purchase a franchise that provides leadership development and management training worldwide.

Chris opened for business in June 2006. His company offers a 12-month training program that helps managers at every level with essential skills for successful business. His training covers issues for upper management—from communication, to negotiation, to delegation, to strategic planning—and subtler matters for people at every level.

In a tough economy, when businesses need to operate as efficiently and cohesively as possible to succeed, the training Chris's business provides can prove vital, and one of the biggest rewards for Chris—a man who has been coaching people of all ages and backgrounds for his entire career—is seeing his participants flourish personally and professionally. Every day is a new opportunity, and the combination of challenge and personal and professional reward keeps him going even in the down times. Being an entrepreneur has given him more control over his own future, and the franchise option gave him the sense of security he needed to make the transition.

The Right Place at the Right Time: Edgar's Story

Edgar bought an existing small business in an established market because he saw a good opportunity. Schools in his area lacked the infrastructure to meet the demand for driver's education, forcing many kids to wait until their junior or senior years to take these classes.

"Waiting until your junior or senior years is not the cool thing to do," Edgar explains. "Plus you have to hold your learner's permit for nine months ... so if you're a junior or senior, you're practically 18 already. The [public] schools don't have the manpower or resources, and the kids get frustrated ... so they come to private schools like ours."

Edgar purchased his small business in March 2009 and already employs nine instructors and a receptionist at his three locations. "The business has exceeded my expectations from a cash-flow standpoint," Edgar says, "and I'm very happy so far."

It helps that Edgar has a background in education and marketing. He holds a bachelor's in marketing and an MBA with a marketing focus. He worked in college admissions as a recruitment officer, and then spent four years as a recruiter for two different automotive schools. "When I saw this opportunity, it went hand in hand with my 11 years of experience recruiting and filling classes for colleges and schools," Edgar says. "While [my company] isn't a college, in many ways it feels the same."

A key to this entrepreneur's success is word-of-mouth marketing. "What impressed me the most was the amount of referral business," explains Edgar. "Parents talk to each other, buddies hang with buddies ... and we get clusters of three or four friends. The previous owner set up a good academic structure and a good base of referral business, and that impressed me. I've extended that with some search-engine marketing, Yellow Pages ads, and a few direct-mail campaigns. But the key is building and extending a solid referral base."

In late 2008 he sold a piece of property and started to look for businesses for sale, independently searching for the right opportunity. Instead of traditional small business financing, he invested his retirement funds into the operation.

More than just a savvy entrepreneur and business owner, Edgar also brings hands-on skills to the table. "I'm a licensed instructor," he says, "and I guess you could call me our fill-in person. If we're really busy, I'll take a route, and if a client demands a particular time slot, I may work with them if my staff can't."

Hands-on skills also form the basis of his expansion plan. "Now that I'm licensed, it's relatively easy to establish operations in other locations. I have the cash flow, so I plan to open up two new locations every year for the next five years."

As the father of two children, Edgar hopes the effort he puts into growing his small business will pay off for his family in the long term. "Right now my kids just think it's cool their father owns a driving school," Edgar says. "If things continue to grow at the pace I anticipate, I hope there will come a time they start to learn about the business."

The Franchise Path to Success: Roy's Story

Twenty years after starting his career as a delivery boy, Roy owns and operates a large Baja Fresh Mexican Grill franchise, which is flourishing, even in this challenging economic environment. He's extremely pleased to be passing on his winning business skills and work ethic to his two children, both attending college in L.A. It's becoming a real family business, as both kids work part-time at the restaurant.

"One of the major reasons we started this venture is so my children could be involved in the business and learn management skills," Ray says. "I wanted to get into a franchise and have structure to it so that not everything had to be learned at once."

A couple of years ago, Roy purchased a Baja Fresh restaurant about 100 miles north of L.A. Instead of letting the sagging economy deter him from purchasing or opening a franchise, he looked for small-business opportunities that had diamond-in-the-rough potential.

"I was looking at trends. I wanted to buy something in a down, depressed market, which is exactly what I did. I used my experience from another business and my creativity and cost-cutting skills to take this business that was down and turn it around," he says.

The reason Roy chose the Baja Fresh franchise was simple—he liked the food. The lure of associating with a superior fast-food product along with the timely opportunity to purchase an existing year-old franchise also helped make Baja Fresh the obvious choice.

Roy is passing valuable experience to his children through his business. Both of Roy's sons work in the restaurant, learning every aspect of the business from the bottom up, including food preparation, sales, marketing, operations, and management responsibilities. They are excited at the prospect of gaining the well-rounded restaurant experience they need to follow and carry on Roy's success.

Roy's franchise operation now employs 12 people, and business is trending upward, despite a couple of slow months recently. That's not bad, considering the current economic downturn, especially in the hard-hit San Joaquin Valley where tough times in the oil and agriculture industries have contributed to a nearly 15 percent unemployment rate.

Being the eternal optimist and opportunist, Roy is using this slight dip in business to get his sons even more involved with the inner workings of small-business entrepreneurship, which he's confident will reap many rewards for their promising young careers.

With their father providing an example of true entrepreneurial enthusiasm, both of Roy's sons are preparing to carve out their own American dream.

Analyzing Your Match: Where's the Profit?

If you now have a short list of possible businesses, it is time to determine which of them will be profitable. Even if you think you've zeroed in on the one perfect option, profitability is still a key concern, and you need to analyze your match to see if it will actually turn a profit.

In the simplest terms, *profit* is what is left once the sale is made and all expenses in that period are paid or accrued for payment. Profit is not to be confused with *cash flow*, which is a separate topic.

Your Financial Plan

It is possible to operate a business without a budget, or financial plan, but it is good business practice to have one. Budgets help you manage cash so that you will make better decisions and have more sustainable and predictable profitability. The need is not as great in times of economic plenty; however, you will be grateful you were disciplined in developing a financial plan when and if leaner times come. Financial plans generally have three key elements: proforma, cash flow, and balance sheet. (For additional detail, see our discussion of business plans in Chapter 10.)

The *proforma* is your educated guess, based on the best assumptions you have about customer buying habits and expected costs, of what the financial performance of your company will look like. Revenue and expense forecasts should be presented on a per-month basis for the first two years, quarterly in years three and four, and yearly for the fifth year. *Cash flow* will show—again, based on an educated guess as you look into the future—when the funds from sales and other sources will come in and when cash needs to be paid out. Negative cash flow will have to be covered with lines of credit or other liquid sources of capital. Your *balance sheet* should accurately represent the assets and liabilities of the company once funded.

Performance Measurements

As part of your planning process up to now, you have created goals, including financial goals, and have become motivated to achieve them. Your financial documents as described in the previous section create the foundation of your financial performance expectations. As current data begin to be reported in the company, they must be compared with projections. *Variance reports* are created so that adjustments can be made. Goals are ineffective if they cannot be measured, so break them down into pieces that can be measured on an ongoing basis. A plan that cannot be measured is almost always destined for failure. If you find your goals are unrealistic and unattainable, adjust them; but also realize that it takes hard work to launch a business, so don't give up easily.

It's important that you really know and understand the contents of your plan, including the performance measurements. Plans are never set in stone; rather, they are living documents that react to market realities. A completed plan is never "complete." Plans are constantly adjusted, added to, and altered.

Refer to your plan often, so you remain on track to building a profitable business. One caveat: If you find that you are regularly making large adjustments to the plan, you must question the validity of the product, market, or other major component of your planning assumptions.

Marketing and Your Business

The idea of marketing is to figure out who your customer is and how to maximally reach that consumer who will buy your product or service. Statistics, demographics, and research all come into play, but first and foremost is defining who your customers are and what their buying habits are. You need to consider questions such as these: Do they shop on the Internet? Are they concerned about price, image, and serviceability?

In the marketing section of your business plan, you will do deep analysis based on the questions of who your customers are, why they buy, and what is the most efficient way to get the product to them. You will also be considering price, features, distribution channels, and promotional strategies as ways to capture the most customers.

Other Considerations

Consider the competition for your idea. If, for instance, you have elected to sell a product or line of products, will you be competing with major discount stores or other well-established businesses in your area? Chances are you will not be able to beat their prices, so do you have another competitive edge, such as better service or products? Even though you might have better products, are consumers willing to pay more for what you offer? While your products might be superior, higher quality might not be foremost in the minds of people in the market for what you sell. Maybe the convenience of buying the products you are considering at a discount store will make competing difficult. As you can see, you need to consider numerous factors for a new business venture.

Eliminate the businesses on your short list that you won't enjoy being involved in. (Keep in mind, though, that as an entrepreneur you will wear many hats and you might not find all roles of any business enjoyable.) On the other hand, do not decide to convert a hobby or an interest into a small business without being absolutely sure a demand exists for what you will be selling.

The Benefit of Your Business

In addition to the "what" (as in what business you choose), consider the question of "why." Whatever business you choose, the benefit of your business—that is, the reason you are in business or the advantage to your customer for doing business with you—should be clear and simple and definable in one sentence. This sentence is not your mission statement, although it might be incorporated into such a statement. This sentence is the reason why people would do business with you—what's in it for them.

With that in mind, try this exercise: Write in one paragraph why your business will exist and why customers would buy.

Providing Benefits to Other Businesses: Gary's Story

Gary owns an expense-reduction consulting firm that helps mid-market companies reduce their indirect expenses through two primary approaches.

As part of a larger affiliate group, Gary helps businesses with $10 million to $300 million in revenue get better pricing by combining their volume with that of other small businesses in the network; in effect, mid-market companies enjoy Fortune 500 pricing. At the same time, he audits invoices to help clients ensure they receive the savings and service promised by vendors and suppliers.

His company's services are provided on a contingency basis. If they can't save their clients money, they don't get paid. "We compare and benchmark pricing, conduct post-audits, and get credits when necessary," Gary explains. "In effect, we're a third-party operational expenses purchasing group." To be successful, Gary works directly with a company's high-level executives. "Some of our best clients are companies where we can deal directly with the president or CFO," he says, "which creates high-level support for cost-containment initiatives. We've also found that mid-market businesses think they're getting good pricing—but in reality they're not. Plus we make sure they get the prices they're promised. Very few companies have the resources to go through every invoice and make sure the price is appropriate against the contract. We do."

"I actually had started looking at other small businesses to buy," Gary says. "I was working with a business broker looking at some brick-and-mortar businesses when this franchise opportunity came along." It was at that point that he began investigating all sorts of franchise financing options.

The economic downturn has been great for Gary's small business—after all, when times are tough, companies look for cost savings wherever possible—but it has also created challenges of its own. Two clients have gone bankrupt, two others are in receivership, and volume is down. Gary says, "An entrepreneur and small-business owner has to readjust and be excited about readjusting. That's the nature of entrepreneurship."

Section III:
Getting Started

Building a Team and Choosing a Business Structure

If all of your thinking, self-assessing, analyzing, and general planning still point you in the direction of entrepreneurship, you're ready to take two important steps to achieving your goal: building a team and choosing a business structure. These activities are critical elements in establishing the foundation for your business.

Building Your Team

While you will want to be *the* expert at your business, having the necessary expertise does not mean you should run your business alone. Every ship has a crew; all sports teams have players in key positions. Once you have chosen your business, you will need to assemble your team—perhaps including some members who don't work on-site with you or are virtual employees. In the beginning, they may even be contractors and consultants to your firm.

In addition to regular employees, contractors, and consultants, your team will include stakeholders such the people who occupy the roles described in the following sections.

Partners

Carefully consider partners and partnerships when you start a business. There may be a practical reason for bringing others into the enterprise, including the need for additional capital, broader expertise or talent, and industry contacts. A wise individual knows his or her limitations, and partnerships should also be complementary, not just for camaraderie. Most people do not have all the skills to take a business from concept to maturity without help. This help may be in the form of sales, operations, finance, IT systems, and more, depending on the business.

Partnerships mean that a piece of the business is owned by others, and that situation can limit your control and, ultimately, decision making. If you do enter into a partnership, the best advice we can offer is to be as clear as possible on how decisions will be made. Follow the rules that cash is king and ownership should be related to investment. Consider stock option plans, and consult an attorney on how a partnership agreement can protect the company in the event of serious disagreement.

Banker

A business-banker relationship can be vital to an entrepreneur even if you're not borrowing any money. Establish a relationship with the institution where you will be doing your banking. And remember that it's always best to build a banking relationship *before* you need money for your enterprise. Sooner or later you will want a line of credit for your business, and it's to your advantage if your banker already knows and respects you.

Business Attorney

Find an attorney—preferably one recommended to you by a businessperson whom you can trust. Many attorneys offer free initial consultations. Interview a few of them, and don't be embarrassed to walk away if the fit just isn't there. Become an educated consumer, and always ask for budgets after you have defined the scope of work.

From the Desk of David Nilssen

My firm was not started with venture funding or any form of debt. We managed cash very closely and financed growth with profits. When we first started, we hired a law firm to help us with the legal aspects of the business. Because the firm wanted our business for the long term, it was willing to adjust its rates significantly below its norm and often would defer bills to help our cash management. We saved a tremendous amount of money. As the years went by and we became more financially sound, we adjusted the rates and began giving the firm more and more work. Our attorney made a great investment in us, and we rewarded him (and his firm) for it. Don't be afraid to ask your professionals to help!

Business Appraiser

Business appraisers may be needed specifically if you are buying an existing business. Professional appraisers receive certifications through several organizations, such as the Institute of Business Appraisers (IBA). The IBA appraises businesses for probate, stock issuing, divorce, tax reasons, and sale. A business appraisal can cost tens of thousands of dollars. A less formal business valuation can cost far less and be sufficient for purchasing a business.

An ideal combination is a business appraiser who is also a business broker or who has worked as one. He or she should be able to provide you with a better idea of valuation than anyone else.

A business broker who is not an appraiser can also provide valuable information about the worth of a business.

Business Broker

A local business broker can be a tremendous asset in your search to purchase an existing business. Brokers will usually have exclusive listing agreements with business owners, so you will see businesses that you would otherwise not know are available. Typically the broker works for, and is paid by, the selling party. Because of confidentiality, many brokers do not share their listings with other brokers, so you might need to visit several business brokers in your area to see everything available for sale. With each broker you visit, you will no doubt be required to sign a confidentiality agreement stating something to the effect that you will not reveal to anyone that the business is for sale. This is common, and make sure you abide by the agreement. Businesses can suffer tremendous losses when customers, vendors, and employees discover a business is for sale—and you could be held liable for any breach.

Make sure your broker is licensed as appropriate in the state where you will do business. Remember, the broker does not work for you and is highly motivated to close a deal.

Business Buyer Reps

Business buyer reps represent buyers of small and mid-sized businesses. Their firms normally engage with a client in the early stages of considering a business acquisition. They help set up the purchase criteria, identify the target businesses, and assist in the negotiation and sometimes financing. An example of these groups would be Partner On Call® (www.partneroncall.com), a network of individuals, each of whom is a Business Buyer Advocate®.

While it is true that many people turn to the Internet to search for their business, it makes sense to use a business buyer rep in certain situations. A business buyer representative can be retained for an upfront fee when an individual wants to buy a specific type of company or for a larger transaction. They work much like the buyer's agent in a real estate transaction (minus the upfront fee).

Business buyer representatives will invest significant time and money to solicit businesses (those not already listed), qualify potential prospects, arrange visits, and put the deal together. Keep in mind that they may do all of this and if you change your mind about buying a business, they are no further ahead. In fact, it has cost them a lot of money. As such, paying them a fee for the solicitation portion of this service is justified.

Richard Parker of the Business Buyer Resource Center (www.diomo.com) suggests that these arrangements turn sour because the buyer has unrealistic expectations about what the "advisor" will deliver. That's why it is critical that you do the following:

- Document precisely what the business buyer rep will be doing to earn all of his or her fees and the time in which it will be done (e.g., four weeks to put together the target list, prepare the letters, follow up with phone calls, etc.).

- Have the rep provide you with several references and contact information of people he or she worked for in a similar capacity. These individuals will surely be able to shed light on the rep's performance, good or bad.

- Have a documented mechanism to terminate the relationship if the rep is not delivering upon what was agreed to.

When all is said and done, if you're looking at a business in the range of $2 million to $10 million, and if the business buyer rep is able to find you the right business and help you negotiate and close the deal, then the fees are probably insignificant relative to the business you will own.

CPA

A CPA will help you establish an accounting system and offer services ranging from keeping your books to reviewing them quarterly and filing tax forms. Establishing an accounting system is a mission-critical priority.

You need to start keeping books the day you decide on a business, because from that day forward you will want to track all of your business expenses and investments. Trying to backtrack and recapture past financial events is very difficult and not productive.

Your CPA can help you choose a software package that tracks online bill paying or that prints checks as you make an entry. By entering your transactions as they occur, you will be able to create profit and loss statements, track sales and inventories, and see a current balance sheet. Many CPAs will help you set up accounting software specifically for your business. Some may have a lower-cost associate who can help you so that you can avoid paying the rates of a more experienced CPA.

Advisors, Coaches, and Networks

Many advising and mentoring organizations offer their services free of charge to new and established small businesses. One particularly active group is SCORE, a nonprofit that helps about 20,000 entrepreneurs yearly. According to SCORE's website (www.score.org), the group has more than 12,400 volunteer business counselors in 364 chapters across the country. These volunteers offer one-on-one coaching—as well as workshops and seminars—dedicated to the formation, growth, and success of small businesses.

America's Small Business Development Center Network is a comprehensive small business assistance network that helps existing businesses remain competitive in the complex marketplace. Hosted by leading universities, colleges, and state economic development agencies, and funded in part through a partnership with the U.S. Small Business Administration, approximately 1,000 service centers are available to provide no-cost business consulting and low-cost training. (For more information, you can visit www.asbdc-us.org.)

The Entrepreneurs' Organization (EO) is a global network of more than 7,300 business owners in 42 countries dedicated to helping entrepreneurs learn and grow from each other. Owners of companies that generate a minimum of $1 million in gross annual revenue, or have taken in venture or angel funding of over $2 million, are eligible to join. They also have an Accelerator Program© that is available to help companies that generate a minimum of $250,000 in gross revenues to grow. Their website (www.eonetwork.org) offers practical tips, advice from experts, and many multimedia opportunities that enable viewers to benefit from the experiences of both new and successful entrepreneurs.

Business coaches are available in today's market, and you should choose one who comes with strong references and evidence of objective performance. You should expect to compensate business coaches for their work with you.

Other organizations that offer free (or nearly free) assistance to small businesses are the Small Business Administration, local Chambers of Commerce, professional associations, and networking groups. And don't forget to conduct informational interviews with those local small-business owners who have been successful at making their own entrepreneurial dreams come true. Just walk in their storefront and ask for an appointment. You'll be surprised by how willing (and even eager!) many of these people are to share their expertise with you.

Business Structures and Business Entities

Once you've decided what kind of enterprise you want, you will need to explore the appropriate structure for it according to state business and tax laws. Here are the six common ways to structure your business:

- Sole proprietorship
- General partnership
- Limited partnership

- C corporation

- S corporation

- Limited liability company (LLC)

Consult with your CPA and attorney before choosing the best structure for your business. Each structure will have a different effect on your company's liability and taxes. Fortunately, business structures aren't set in stone, so they can be changed or modified based on the future needs of your company.

Remember that your company will be subject to state business laws, fees, taxes, and regulations. Because some states are friendlier than others to small businesses, entrepreneurs often select states other than their home state in which to file their documents establishing their new business. At the end of this chapter, we've inserted a table that will help you compare the pros and cons of various business entities.

 From the Desk of Jeff Levy

Accountants or CPAs are often in the best position to recommend which entity is best for you, as they will be your advisor at tax time. My advice is to prepare to discuss with your accountant your expectation of what the financial performance of the company will look like over the next five years, how many shareholders it might have, and what your exit strategy consists of. An accountant will be able to ask you some specific questions and make a recommendation about the best structure to choose. By following this recommendation, you're minimizing your chance of making a profound mistake.

Sole Proprietor

A sole proprietorship is a business owned by one person, and it presents the most liability. Legally, there is no difference between the owner and the operation. You would be personally and legally responsible for all debts and liabilities of the business. Check with your attorney to see if it would be in your best interest to file a "fictitious name" statement, which would equate to "YOUR NAME doing business as (dba) XYZ COMPANY."

General and Limited Partnerships

A partnership is a business agreement between two or more partners to engage in a business. The partners make individual contributions of money, property, labor, or skill, and then they share in the profits and losses of the business accordingly. This arrangement is usually described as a "partnership agreement" or "declaration of partnership."

The people involved in a general partnership are responsible for management of the business and are personally liable for any debts.

Although similar to a general partnership, a limited partnership demands that only one partner be defined as a "general" partner. The remaining "limited" partners are paid a return on their investment by the general partner(s). They have no management authority and are liable only for business debts in proportion to their financial investment in the partnership.

Because limited partners are not personally liable for any company debts and can passively invest in an enterprise without involvement in the day-to-day running of it, a limited partnership is often used by companies wishing to invest in other businesses.

Corporation

A corporation is a legal entity in and of itself. Although it can have any number of officers, directors, and stockholders, the corporation has its own legal rights and responsibilities. It can hire employees, sign contracts, borrow money, govern internal affairs, and maintain assets separate from those of its owners. Corporations can also be sued.

When creating a corporation, "articles of incorporation" or a "certificate of incorporation" is publicly filed in the state in which the corporation is formed. The corporation then issues ownership "shares" to "shareholders" who buy into, or invest in, the business.

Shares can be either "common" or "preferred." Holders of shares of common stock have equal rights to vote on corporation matters and are entitled to the same percentage of corporation distributions as the percentage of shares they hold. Holders of "preferred" stock, as the name implies, have special rights that protect the interests of investors. For example, some corporations choose to give holders of preferred stock the privilege of getting their money back first if the business is sold.

Because stockholders own the company, they are responsible for approving major decisions, choosing a board of directors, electing corporate officers, and holding director and shareholder meetings. They also create the "bylaws" that govern the corporation's behavior. Keep in mind that states set up the rules for governing corporations, and those laws must be adhered to carefully.

For tax purposes only, there are two types of corporations—C and S.

C Corporation. A C corporation pays taxes separate from its stockholders. The corporation is a separate legal entity, and if it is adequately capitalized and proper corporate formalities are followed, the shareholders should have liability protection from its debts and obligations. The corporation can use corporate benefit health plans, which often offer better retirement options and benefits than those offered by noncorporate plans. In a C corporation, 100 percent of health insurance offered for all employees, as well as group term life insurance up to a specified amount per employee, is deductible. If you think you may have to raise capital, then you will likely need to start as a C corporation. It's easier to raise capital as a corporation than as a sole proprietorship or partnership.

This structure does have some disadvantages. Besides paying corporate income taxes, any dividends to shareholders are taxed again at the applicable tax rate. Bonuses, however, are not double-taxed, and this avenue is often how the shareholders reward management for great outcomes. The formalities and regulations must be followed very closely in conjunction with the laws regarding incorporating in a specific state.

C corporations can be powerful tools for shifting income because that income is taxed separately—apart from the individual stockholders.

S Corporation. An S corporation is created like a C, except for one factor: its owners elect with the IRS to be characterized as a "subchapter S corporation," which entitles the corporation and its shareholders to some excellent tax benefits. For starters, they're not subject to double taxation (like the C corporation). Earnings of the S corporation are taxed only once—at the time they're earned; and the stockholders, not the corporation, pay taxes on the earnings. When earnings are later distributed to stockholders as dividends, no additional taxes need to be paid. Furthermore, the shareholders of S corporations can use their losses to reduce their taxable income.

Not surprisingly, some very precise requirements must be met to be able to take advantage of S corporation tax benefits. For one thing, only a limited amount of losses can be deducted by stockholders who are not actively running the business. This makes it less attractive to passive investors. Also, as a rule, only people (not business entities) can own S corporations, and only common (not preferred) stock can be issued.

Here's something, however, for new businesses to consider: a new corporation can form initially as an S corporation if it doesn't expect an influx of financing in the near future. In this way, it can enjoy the S corporation tax treatment until more money comes in. Then, at that time, it can re-form as a C corporation.

Limited Liability Company

A limited liability company (LLC) is similar to a corporation, although it has more flexibility when it comes to structure and ownership. Similar to corporations, LLCs are filed with the state, and the liability of their owners is limited. LLCs are organized by "articles of organization" or "rules of organization," and, unlike corporations, they do not require a board of directors or the holding of owners' meetings.

Owners of LLCs are referred to as "members," and most states do not restrict members to being actual people. This means that corporations, other LLCs, and/or foreign entities can own all or part of an LLC. In most states, an individual can set up an LLC. (Depending on individual state laws, there are some types of businesses that can't be structured as LLCs.)

For tax purposes, an LLC is generally viewed as a partnership, which includes some excellent tax benefits for owners—very similar, in fact, to the benefits of an S corp, but without all the restrictions. In most cases, an LLC can distribute noncash assets to members without triggering taxes.

Start-up companies are often formed first as LLCs and are later converted to a corporation.

From the Desk of David Nilssen

While most tax professionals prefer S corporations or LLCs for start-ups, an interesting letter was sent to me in 2009 that shows one professional's thoughts as to why a C corp was the most beneficial entity for small businesses. While I offer no opinion on whether I agree or disagree, I do believe it's interesting reading and should be evaluated by you and your tax professional. Here's what he said in the letter:

Unfortunately most individuals that have a corporation (and also 75% of accountants and attorneys who are too lazy to put some effort in on behalf of their clients) treat it simply as a sole proprietorship. In other words, the old example of "All I want to do is drive the car, I don't want to know or learn how it's engineered" seems to be the guiding principle. How often have we heard, "I am an excellent _____, but I don't want to get involved in the bookkeeping"?

When choosing a business entity, there is no simple answer or free lunch. The IRS is going to get taxes out of you one way or another. Therefore the goal is to minimize your taxable income. To do this you MUST be actively involved in the design and implementation of your entity to achieve the end results you have planned for yourself. This is something that you have to do in conjunction with an actively participating tax advisor (whether tax attorney or tax accountant—note, I said tax ahead of each one implying not a general practitioner whose main emphasis is everything including tax issues when the subject comes up).

There is a real trap in the S-corps (also known in some circles as the lazy person's corporation). That trap is that any and all profit is passed directly through from the S-corp to your personal tax return. For example, whatever tax bracket your last dollar was taxed at (hypothetically let's just say it was 25%), then all the profit (whether distributed to you or not) from the S-corporation is taxable at the remainder of that tax bracket and above as you move upward depending on the amount of profit. You do not have a choice. It is an all-in situation on your tax return, which is also known as tax stacking.

There are also many other restrictions that Congress and the IRS are still putting in place such as requiring certain corporate earnings percentages to be classified as W-2 wages, thus making them subject to Medicare and Social Security (a way of quietly adding an additional 15.3% tax on income). Finally S-corporations have multiple restrictions eliminating everything from certain deductions to what types of individuals can invest or be shareholders in your S-corporation. These cover everything from health care and fringe benefit deductions to non-United States citizen shareholders.

Don't get me wrong, the S-corporation has its place as a tool when used properly. As an example I use it actively in tax planning when we know in advance that someone is getting ready to close their C-corporation in a few years and has large losses on the books. We then strategize the conversion to an S-corporation so that when it is time to close, those losses are passed through to the individual in the final year instead of being lost as they would be if it remained a C-corporation. (Another example of why the professional has to be active and fluent in entities to make things work to best advantage at the right time.)

On the other hand, when planned to be used correctly, the C-corporation will provide the better tax advantages 95% or more of the time. As with all things, there are exceptions to the rule, but again active and proper planning is the key to using the right tool and the right time.

I agree that if utilized, dividends do represent a double taxation issue. Dividends are the ONLY form of distribution from a corporation that is double taxed. Therefore it should not be used except as a last resort when the other dozen or so methods of creating passive income to the shareholder have been exhausted. I don't want to muddy the waters here, but even under the right circumstances, taking a distribution as wages may be more tax preferable than either receiving money as a dividend or passed through via an S-corporation.

Again, you want to work with a tax professional who will be actively involved and interweave many strategies and a review process, rather than the "just a set-it-up and let it run hands off" philosophy. It is kind of like the difference between a concert pianist and someone who buys a piano and sets it up in their living room. The latter knows it's there and occasionally sits down to plink out a tune with one finger. But they never get the full benefit of that beautiful piano unless someone else plays it. On the other hand, the concert pianist sits down and plays beautiful music using all ten fingers, the foot pedals, and all the keys in chords and melodies.

A few simplified examples of this that I can give you are: (1) The setting up of passive income sources that are deductible to the C-corporation (and yes I am talking about options precluded in S-corporations) and only taxed at the individual level as ordinary passive income (not subject to Medicare or Social Security), (2) The use of offsetting accounting methods (cash vs. accrual) pitting one type of income or deduction in a tax return against the opposing tax return, and/or (3) The ability to use the C-corporation as a gateway to release or hold monies based on each year's tax profile analysis (as opposed to a S-corporation which has an all in mandate).

Hopefully without getting too complex or burying you I have answered your question. If not, feel free to give me a call so we can better discuss this.

This letter is not intended as tax advice and you should consult with your own professional before deciding on what type of business entity to choose.

Which Structure Is Best for You?

When determining which structure would best meet your needs, consider the following factors:

- Your own personal assets and liabilities
- Your existing capital and need for outside investors
- Your ability to attract outside investors
- State licensing, statutes, and tax requirements
- The time commitment necessary to handle regulations and formalities
- The size, scope, and type of business you're starting
- Start-up costs, including licensing and other fees
- Exit strategy (when it's time to sell your business)

It bears repeating: Choosing the wrong legal entity for your business can create unnecessary expense and administrative headaches. We strongly recommend you work with a qualified tax professional to choose the entity that is best for you.

Advantages and Disadvantages of C Corporations, S Corporations, and LLCs

C Corporations—Advantages	C Corporations—Disadvantages
Venture capital funds and many angel investors will require, or at least strongly prefer, a corporation.	Double taxation on income: taxed on its own earnings, and shareholders are taxed on distributions.
Most familiar and effective entity for granting stock or stock options across an employee base.	No loss flow-through: Losses in a C corporation cannot be deducted until the C corporation has offsetting income.
Can be sold "tax-deferred" for shares of an acquiring corporation.	Corporate formalities: Corporations must comply with many statutory requirements, including annual stockholder and director meetings and stockholder approval of key transactions. Failure to comply may allow creditors to reach stockholder assets to recover debts.
Can issue preferred stock to investors.	
No limitations on types of investors.	
Most familiar entity type to capital markets and financing sources.	

S Corporations—Advantages	S Corporations—Disadvantages
Pass-through taxation: No separate tax (usually) on S corporations, only their shareholders.	An S corporation must comply with the same corporate formalities as a C corporation.
Loss flow-through: An S corporation's losses flow through to the individual stockholders' tax returns. (Note: The "passive activity rules" limit this benefit for most investors.)	An S corporation must meet the many requirements for retaining its special tax status, including having as stockholders only individual or qualifying trusts or estates, and also that it have only one class of stock.
An S corporation has flexibility in exit strategy, familiarity to capital markets, and the ability to grant stock and stock options just like its C corporation counterpart.	

LLC Advantages	LLC Disadvantages
Flexibility in management, equity, and allocation of profits and losses.	More complex business form than S corporation and more complex tax accounting rules.
Lack of most corporate formalities.	Members may be subject to self-employment taxes.
Pass-through taxation. (Note: Some states do impose certain separate taxes on the LLC.)	Cannot engage in tax-deferred reorganizations with corporate acquirers.
Losses flow through, just like an S corporation, and the same passive loss limitations apply to investors.	Not good for issuance of options because of complicated accounting and tax rules.
An LLC may distribute appreciated property, such as real estate, tax free.	Not a form regularly chosen by high-growth tech start-ups.
No restriction on the number or types of members.	

10

Your Business Plan

You may have heard the old saying "Failure to plan is a plan for failure." This is especially true in a small business. A business plan serves as a dynamic document ("dynamic" because you should revisit and refresh it every six months) for informing what must be done to ensure your success.

Most financing institutions, such as banks, require a business plan, and every business should have one. The process of developing a comprehensive business plan will provide you with invaluable information, educate you, serve as a guide, and spark your business creativity. Even if you do not need a business plan for financing, we strongly recommend you go through the rigor and discipline of business planning.

No matter how extensive a business plan might be, it is a working document. While your goals may remain constant, your course can change. Navigating your business will require flexibility. As you begin running your operations, you can take actual performance numbers, compare them against your plan, and make adjustments for future expected results.

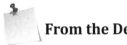

From the Desk of Jeff Levy

When I managed the domestic operations of Safeworks LLC we had 25 offices. Each had the responsibility to submit a business plan for the upcoming year. Invariably some managers tried to make the case that they "will always work hard and the results will be what they will be. No one can predict the future, and planning is a waste of time." They missed the essence of business planning, and we had to have some serious discussion on what they could do to better predict the future of their operations.

Getting Started

"The right time comes when one is ready."
—Carl G. Jung

As a working document, a business plan will help you focus on the things that are most important to your business and think through the assumptions that will drive the business. Without a plan, you are likely to experience greater challenges because you will be operating without focus.

While writing your plan, you might run into issues that you did not initially consider. That's OK, because the thinking and writing will have better prepared you for various possibilities.

Your business plan will also become invaluable when and if you need to raise capital for your business. And in the future, it will become a gauge for your progress.

Begin developing your plan by answering these broad questions:

- What are my goals for the business?
- What do I need to do to reach those goals?

- What or who can help me achieve those goals?

- What can I do to overcome foreseen obstacles?

- How will I know if I am on track to achieving my goal?

Once you've considered these foundational questions, begin collecting all the information you can to develop a comprehensive plan that will help you reach your goals. If you are starting a new business, much of your plan will be based on educated guesses, including financial projections, which we discuss later in this chapter. You should cast best, worst, and middle-of-the-road projections.

To help you get started and to give you an idea of some of the specific elements of a typical business plan, here is a general outline:

1. Introduction (Executive Summary)

    A. Detailed description of the business and your vision for its future

    B. Organizational structure of the business and ownership

    C. Skills and experience you and any partners can contribute to the business

    D. The edge your business has over competitors

    E. Return to shareholders

2. Marketing

    A. Products and/or services offered

    B. Customer demand

    C. Distribution methods

    D. Market size and locations

    E. Advertising

    F. Pricing

3. Financial Management
   A. Source and amount of initial investment
   B. Monthly operating budget
   C. Monthly expected cash flow
   D. Projected income statements and balance sheets
   E. Breakeven point
   F. Compensation
   G. Accounting practices
   H. Alternative approaches to any anticipated roadblocks

4. Operations
   A. Day-to-day management
   B. Hiring and personnel procedures
   C. Insurance, lease or rent agreements
   D. Necessary equipment for production
   E. Delivery of products and/or services

5. Concluding Statement
   A. Business goals and objectives
   B. Commitment to success
   C. Risk section

Business Planning Assumptions for Key Areas

As you can see from the suggested outline, preparing a business plan involves thinking carefully about several specific and key aspects of your enterprise, including start-up capital, customers, competitors, estimated sales, and likely market share. The following sections provide some guidance for each of these specific areas.

Estimate Start-up Capital

The estimated amount of start-up capital should be based on initial costs and a forecast of income and expenses for five years or the term of the loan you are seeking. Mark your predicted breakeven point. While lenders want to know how they will be getting repaid, you need some idea of how and when you can meet your living expenses. The breakeven point is when revenue exceeds expenses on a consistent basis. This should be calculated without paying yourself. Owner's compensation is somewhat arbitrary and can dramatically affect the profitability of the business. Look for the owner's discretionary income—what you can pay yourself and charge legally to the business if it was past breakeven and supporting its operations.

Create a Customer Profile

Research and describe who your customers are or will be, why they buy, when they buy, how they buy, and where they are located. Describe your target group by income, age, gender, location, interests, and buying habits.

Create a Competitor Profile

Find out who your main competitors are or will be and create profiles on each one; list their locations, sales volumes, traffic patterns, hours of operation, busy periods, prices, quality of their goods and services, websites, promotions, and brochures. List the strengths and weaknesses of each one and how your business compares to them. State what you will do differently or better. Will you offer a better location, more convenience, and lower price, be more accessible, and offer better quality or better service?

Estimate First-Year Sales

Predict as realistically as possible how much you expect in revenue for the first year of your projections. This involves sales forecasting—predicting what your sales will be for a specific period of time. There are sophisticated formulas as well as less complex methods for sales forecasting. When you sell different types of products and services, you will want to create a separate sales forecast for each one.

When making your forecast, consider your "sales funnel." How many "suspects" do you need to talk with or reach to convert them into customers? And consider all the factors that can affect your sales, such as the following:

- Seasonality
- Holidays and special events
- Competition
- Product availability
- Personal issues
- Economic climate
- Population changes
- Political events
- Price elasticity
- Product changes
- Promotional effort changes
- Sales incentives
- Price changes
- Shortages/working capital
- Distribution
- Credit policy changes
- Labor issues

Sales forecasting is an art, not a science. It is a difficult process, yet doing it correctly is a key to understanding the business's future potential. The numbers you input will affect almost every aspect of your company. Make the best assumptions you can with the data you have.

Estimate Market Share

Estimate the dollar volume of your total market and your market-share projection. State your share of the total market as an annual percentage and a dollar amount. Divide this total volume by the average sales you would expect to make per customer in one year. The result will be the number of customers you will need to obtain that market share. Do the numbers look feasible? Also, have you considered the "addressable" market compared to the total market? For example, everyone needs shoes and socks. However, you would not consider your market to be the population of the world times two. Your entire market will need to be analyzed in detail on customer type, buying habits, location, demographics, and a myriad of other factors.

Here are the simple formulas to use once you have your "addressable" market share goals:

- *Total Market Value* (in money) multiplied by the *Percentage of Expected Market Share* equals *Total Revenue Forecast*

- *Total Revenue Forecast* divided by *Average Sale per Customer* equals *Total Customers*

Projecting Cash Flow

The business assumptions discussed in the preceding section all have an impact on your cash flow, which is a critical part of your business plan. Simply stated, cash flow is how money moves in and out of your business. The solvency of your business is determined by your cycle of cash movement. And keep in mind that sales and cash receipts may not be the same if you extend credit or have aging receivables.

There are three parts to cash flow projection. The first part details your "cash revenues" or income. This is where you enter the total estimated cash you expect to collect each month. The second part is "cash disbursements." These are the expenses you expect to pay each month. The third part of the cash flow projection is the "reconciliation of cash revenues to cash disbursements." This section starts with the opening balance, the carryover from the previous month.

The current month's revenues are added to this balance; the current month's disbursements are subtracted; and the adjusted cash flow balance is carried over to the next month.

Cash flow analysis is about examining what affects your cash flow. This includes examining accounts receivable, inventory, accounts payable, interest, and credit terms. An analysis of these separate elements helps you see issues and make improvements.

One way to perform a cash flow analysis is to compare the outstanding money owed or unpaid bills to the total expected sales collected at the end of each month. When the bills are more than the total sales due, your business will require more cash than you receive and you will have a cash flow shortage.

On your business plan, a cash flow projection will give you a much better idea of how much capital investment your business needs.

Cash flow projection also estimates your credit risk. Business plan cash flow projections should be shown monthly for a three- to five-year period.

✳ ✳ ✳

Despite all the calculations and components, business plans do not need to be complicated documents. Your business plan should use simple terms and be easy to read. Read other business plans so you will know exactly what to include before you begin. You can download a sample plan at the Small Business Association website (www.SBA.org).

The bottom line on business plans is simple: they are well worth the effort. They provide the blueprint you need to build a successful enterprise and signal the seriousness of your intent.

11

Financing Your Small Business

Deciding how to finance a small business is nearly as important as deciding on the right idea, the right concept, the right industry, and even the right location. Obtaining capital at a high cost can impair your business's ability to grow. On the other hand, choosing the right method and form of financing can greatly improve your chances for success.

There are several basic financing choices. In this chapter we'll look at traditional debt financing, such as business loans, as well as unique ways to use your own personal equity, such as investing your retirement funds in a small business—and yes, it can be done. Our intent is not to sway your decision. Instead, our goal is to provide an objective overview of the pros and cons of each method and show you how you can use specific strategies to purchase the business or franchise of your choice.

The key is to choose the small-business financing and investing option (or options) right for you and your unique needs. Let's start by reviewing the more traditional and widely used (at least historically speaking) form of financing: debt financing.

Debt Financing

A number of debt-financing techniques are available for small-business purchases. Here are the most common:

- Home equity loans
- Small Business Administration (SBA) loans
- Unsecured loans
- Peer-to-peer lending

We'll start with home equity loans, a technique we have seen more entrepreneurs use over the last five years than any other financing tool.

Home Equity Loans

It's easy to understand why home equity loans are a popular way to finance a small business. Home equity loans are relatively inexpensive—especially in the past few years—and allow tremendous flexibility in terms of how funds are used.

There are two basic types of loans based on the equity built up in your home: (1) a home equity loan and (2) a home equity line of credit. Both assume you have equity in the home to start with; so if your home is worth $400,000 and your mortgage balance is $390,000, you have very little equity, making this an irrelevant financing option.

Home Equity Loan. A home equity loan is like most other types of loans: in return for security or collateral—in this case, the home—the homeowner is given a sum of money. For example, if you take a home equity loan of $100,000, the lender gives you a check for $100,000 that you can then invest in the business. A home equity loan is often referred to as a "cash-out refinance" since the borrower "takes cash out" of his or her home equity. Because rates and terms vary, make sure you talk to a mortgage professional and that you thoroughly understand the pros and cons of fixed-rate versus variable-rate loans, as well as all the different loan term options available.

In most cases, homeowners are allowed to borrow up to 80 percent of the value of their home. If you own a home worth $100,000 and have an outstanding mortgage balance of $50,000, a lender may let you borrow up to $40,000.

A key fact to remember about a home equity loan is that it is considered an installment loan. In the example above, you will immediately start paying interest on the $40,000, regardless of when you actually spend or invest that money.

Home Equity Line of Credit. A home equity line of credit is similar to a home equity loan, because the loan is secured by the underlying real estate. The key difference is that a home equity line works like a credit card: you can draw from the line and only pay interest on the amount you owe; as you pay down the loan, you can draw more. In effect, a home equity line is like revolving credit—money flows in and out.

One disadvantage of home equity lines is that, because they offer greater flexibility in terms of timing, they almost always come with adjustable interest rates. (When you think about it, this makes sense, since the lender can adjust the interest rate to match prevailing market conditions.)

Home equity loans and lines are an attractive financing option. But, for a couple of reasons, they are less common today than they once were. First, the lending industry as a whole is under considerable pressure, and qualifying for loans is much more difficult than it was a few years ago. Second, home values have dropped considerably in many parts of the country, causing "paper equity" to disappear. Additionally, many people have already used up the equity in their homes.

On the positive side, home equity is extremely inexpensive, costing approximately 1 percent of the home value for a refinance and approximately $1,000 to open a home equity line of credit. Home equity financing is also tax deductible; the interest paid is deductible as long as the loan and the value of the home meet certain basic conditions.

Key Considerations:

- Variable interest rates carry risk. Currently, interest rates are low; many people feel rates have nowhere to go but up. If you take out an adjustable-rate loan, factor in the possibility of higher interest rates—and monthly payments—if interest rates do rise significantly.

- The bank determines the amount of the loan. The loan amount is based on a percentage of the appraised home value. If you don't have enough equity, you may not be able to generate sufficient funds.

- Your home serves as collateral for the loan or line of credit. The bank can take possession of your home if you default on payments.

- Payments are made on a monthly basis and factor into your overall expenses. The monthly payment should be included in your business (or personal income) expenses. For example, a $125,000 home equity loan at 7 percent, amortized over 15 years, will result in monthly payments of approximately $1,100, or over $13,000 annually.

Small Business Administration (SBA) Loans

First, let's dispel a myth. The SBA does not make loans. Banks lend the money. The SBA *guarantees* the loan. That guarantee helps the bank feel comfortable providing a new business owner with cash.

Generally speaking, typical terms include a 25 percent down payment, amortized over a 10-year period (unless real estate is attached to the loan). The amortization period may be shorter, but 10 years is common.

At the time of this writing, interest rates on SBA-guaranteed loans were averaging approximately 6.5 percent; several years ago rates were as high as 8 to 9 percent. Rates change as the interest rate and lending market change; so the cost of capital could swing significantly. SBA-guaranteed loan amounts can be as high as $5 million. There are 32 determining factors for loan approval, but generally speaking, the following factors are the most critical:

- **Sound business model.** The SBA will evaluate your business plan to assess your likelihood of success.

- **Down payment.** Do you have the cash to provide a 25 percent down payment?

- **Credit score.** In today's lending environment, banks are extremely wary of lending to people with a credit score under 680. Even though the SBA will guarantee the loan, banks still want to feel comfortable that you are a solid credit risk.

- **Other collateral.** In some cases, you can provide additional collateral, therefore creating less risk for the lender.

Keep in mind: If you need capital quickly, SBA-guaranteed loans can take up to 90 days to process. If you find a business or franchise to purchase, negotiate enough time into the purchase agreement to allow for loan processing.

Key Considerations:

- SBA-guaranteed loans require a sizable down payment.

- SBA-guaranteed loans are easier to qualify for if fully collateralized. Banks will seek as much security on the loan as possible; again, that minimizes their downside risk.

- When your home serves as collateral for an SBA-guaranteed loan, the bank can and will take possession of your home if you default on payments. This means that if your business fails, you may lose your home as well.
- Interest rates are variable. Your payments may increase over time if interest rates rise.
- Amortization is usually based on 10 years. Even though the interest rate for an SBA-guaranteed loan could be lower compared to, say, a home equity loan, the monthly payment will be higher due to a shorter amortization period.

Unsecured Loans

Interest in unsecured loans is on the upswing for two main reasons: unsecured loans are available only to people with excellent credit, and the loans can be approved very, very quickly. Unsecured loans come in two basic types: signature loans and signature lines of credit.

Similar to home equity financing, signature loans are installment loans, with the borrower paying interest on the entire amount as soon as the loan is granted. Signature lines are a form of revolving credit, requiring interest on only the "used" portion of the credit line. And just like a home equity line of credit, a signature line can be drawn from, repaid, and drawn from again.

A key difference is that unsecured loans do not require collateral; qualification and approval is strictly credit-score dependent. If you have a proven, long-term track record of responsible credit use and are financially capable of making the payments on the amount you borrow, unsecured loans can be a great option.

But to qualify for an unsecured loan, in most cases your credit score must be over 700; the higher the better.

In addition, your credit utilization percentage must be lower than 40 percent. Think of a credit utilization percentage as the ratio between the credit available to you and the credit you currently use. For example, say you have a credit card with a limit of $10,000; if you currently carry a $3,000 balance; your credit utilization is 30 percent. To calculate your credit utilization percentage, simply add up all the credit you currently use and divide by the total of your available credit.

If you have had any derogatory credit entries in the past five years—late payments, bankruptcies, tax liens, or other major credit "dings"—you will not be approved. On the other hand, if you do qualify, the average borrower can receive up to $125,000 for a start-up and up to $250,000 for an existing business—and gain approval relatively quickly. In fact, we've seen unsecured loans funded in as little as 10 days, although the average is closer to 30 days and sometimes longer.

Key Considerations:

- Interest rates will be relatively high. Since the lender does not require collateral, the interest rate on an unsecured loan will be higher in order to compensate the lender for taking on greater risk.

- Origination fees may be exceptionally high. (Same reason as above.)

- One lender may not be able to provide the entire amount you need to finance the small-business purchase. Typically, entrepreneurs work with several banks to generate sufficient capital. Often entrepreneurs will work with a lending broker who has relationships with banks and can facilitate the loan process.

- Be aware that if you go online to get an unsecured loan, you will likely be applying through a broker, not the lender. In that case, the broker may take your application to five or more banks at the same time. As a result of numerous credit inquiries, your credit score could drop in a matter of days—possibly below the lending threshold, simply due to credit inquiries.

- Also note that some brokers may manipulate your data. We have seen instances where brokers "massaged" borrower data to help loans gain approval. Make sure you review all applications before they are sent to any banks.

The upside of unsecured loans is quick approval, no collateral required, and fast funding. But there are downsides as well, depending on the terms of the loan you receive.

Most unsecured loans are amortized over a five-year period, making monthly payments relatively high. Interest rates can be incredibly high, often averaging 15 percent or more. The combination of high interest rates and short amortization periods can create monthly payments high enough to significantly impact the feasibility of your small business, especially if you are not able to generate cash flow relatively quickly. And if that happens, a major portion of the capital you borrow might go toward servicing your unsecured debt.

One other factor: unsecured debt will appear as a revolving credit line on your credit report; in effect it looks just like credit card debt. Say you are approved for a $70,000 loan and borrow that amount; the credit report entry will show that you are using $70,000, therefore dramatically increasing your credit utilization ratio (since in this case your credit utilization ratio will be 100 percent).

If you decide to pursue an unsecured loan, make it either your primary financing vehicle or the last vehicle you employ to pull your entire financing package together. Otherwise, if you apply for an unsecured loan first, you may not be able to qualify for other types of financing simply because of a poor credit utilization ratio.

Peer-to-Peer Loans

Peer-to-peer loans are a relatively new small-business-financing vehicle, and already a few peer-to-peer loan communities are flourishing online. Here's how it works. Peer-to-peer platforms are composed of a collection of investors who make loans available to borrowers. In effect, each investor is considered a "micro-lender." Let's say you fill out a peer-to-peer loan application asking for $5,000. Even more important than asking for a certain amount of money is stating *why* you want the funds.

The more information you provide, the better, since individual investors will evaluate the opportunity and decide whether or not they wish to participate. Micro-lenders in the peer-to-peer community can then contribute—invest their money—for a portion of that $5,000 loan. In theory (and we realize this example is a bit extreme), 100 different micro-lenders could all contribute $50 each, therefore fully funding your loan.

The result is a win-win. You receive funding; micro-lenders invest in an opportunity but take on less individual risk, since their contribution only makes up a portion of the entire loan. Plus, you make one payment per month; the peer-to-peer community is responsible for distributing payments to participating micro-lenders.

Interest rates for peer-to-peer loans are relatively high. If you have a solid credit score, your loan may come in at approximately 12 to 15 percent; in some cases it could be "bid down" to as low as 9 to 10 percent.

Peer-to-peer lending is an effective form of small-business financing. David is a lender on a platform and has found it to be a great way to invest in people—and for those people to acquire the capital they need to fund their projects.

Key Considerations:

- Peer-to-peer loans are unsecured loans; funding can take place relatively quickly—even as quickly as a week or two.

- Peer-to-peer loans show up as revolving credit on your credit report and can dramatically affect your credit utilization ratio.

- Funding is not guaranteed. Whether or not your loan request is funded depends on your credit score, your business plan, and the peer-to-peer community's willingness to fund your proposal.

- Amortization is on a three-year basis. As a result, monthly payments are very high. Your ability to service monthly payments must be built into your overall financial model.

As with unsecured loans, peer-to-peer loans should either be your primary form of financing or the last piece in your financing puzzle to ensure that any changes in your credit utilization ratio do not dramatically affect your ability to qualify for other forms of financing.

Now that we've covered the basic types of traditional small-business financing, let's look at how you can use up to 100 percent of the funds in your IRA or 401(k) to purchase a small business or franchise—without taking a taxable distribution.

Retirement Plans: A Nontraditional Source of Capital

Buying a small business or franchise using retirement funds may sound like some far-fetched idea, but it is not. Tens of thousands of American small-business owners feel that investing their IRA or 401(k) funds in a new business is a better way to use and grow their retirement accounts than investing in mutual funds.

In addition, this technique creates an ongoing 401(k) plan within the company they launch, allowing for additional contributions and tax-deferred growth. And because the acquisition of the business is actually an *investment* by the retirement fund, the money that's used is not considered an early distribution or subject to penalties and tax.

Many entrepreneurs believe this form of investing provides them a strategic advantage over other small-business owners because it allows them to purchase a small business with reduced—or even zero—debt. It allows the business's initial cash flow to be reinvested into the business instead of being sent to a bank in the form of monthly loan and interest payments. In other words, you could start a business with much lower overhead and use the money you save to buy office equipment, advertising, signage, and so forth.

Because this concept is relatively new to most people—and quite possibly new to you as well—we'll start by explaining the basic process.

The Basic Steps

- Use a qualified, experienced third-party administrator to set up the plan.

- Establish a C corporation. The process starts by creating a legal business entity; this entity must be a C corporation, not an S corporation. Consider this C corporation *your company.*

- Establish a qualifying company 401(k). The 401(k) explicitly provides for the plan to hold private stock in this type of company.

- Roll up to 100 percent of your existing 401(k) funds into the new company 401(k) plan. This can come from an IRA, 401(k), 401(b), SEP IRA, Keogh, or other tax-deferred retirement vehicle.

- Use the funds in the new plan to purchase company stock. In other words, that new 401(k) *invests* in the company you established. *In return, your company is able to use those funds to purchase a business or franchise, cover its day-to-day operations, and so on.*

In effect, the transaction is similar to buying a publicly traded stock. For example, if you purchase Microsoft stock, you receive partial ownership in Microsoft in exchange for your investment. If the business does well, the value of the stock rises—and so does the value of the 401(k) that owns the stock. If the business performs poorly, the value of those shares decreases.

Because the 401(k) is company-sponsored, you and your employees can contribute a portion of your wages to the plan, and the company can provide profit sharing or matching contributions—just like with any other 401(k).

The Pros and Cons

When this is done correctly and according to the ERISA laws, the result could provide a phenomenal opportunity for you to (1) invest retirement funds in a business you control, (2) provide an outstanding employee benefit for you and your employees in the form of a 401(k) plan, and (3) go into business without the burden of loans and interest payments that most small-business owners bear.

Keep in mind that this form of small-business investing is a strategic wealth-building strategy. It provides value greater than simply enabling the purchase of a small business. By using this financing option, you gain the following advantages:

- **Your retirement funds can grow in a variety of ways.** Not only can the value of the business—and the retirement plan—increase in value, but if you sell all or a portion of the business, the money earned goes to the retirement plan—and you own stock in that plan.

- **You can make future contributions.** As you pay yourself a salary, you can elect to defer a significant amount of your compensation to the plan.

- **You can receive profit sharing and contribution matching,** therefore maximizing the return on your contributions, if the company chooses to provide such benefits to the staff.

From a business point of view, this business-investing process can also offer a faster track to profitability. Why? While traditional financing automatically creates a monthly debt obligation, using retirement funds to finance a business purchase creates *no debt*—and no monthly debt obligation. Say you invest $100,000 in retirement funds in the business. You can use those funds without needing to make monthly payments that drain operating capital and cash flow. Profitability, as a result, is much quicker to achieve since operating expenses are significantly reduced.

But on the other hand ... some businesses fail. If that happens, you could lose part or all of your investment—meaning the loss of your retirement funds. So keep the following points in mind:

- **You must believe strongly that the business will succeed.** Otherwise, why would you purchase the business in the first place?

- **You should consider using less than 100 percent of your retirement funds.** That way you diversify your retirement plan investments as well as your risk. If you are unsuccessful, you can lose part or all of the funds invested. While there are no taxes due on a failed investment, it can be devastating to individuals who invested most of their retirement funds into an unsuccessful business.

- **You must believe strongly in your ability to lead the business,** since you will be a day-to-day, tactical employee.

Also keep in mind that, while there is no debt service, your 401(k) plan will need to be administered. The administration cost typically starts at $99 a month. *However, depending on the amount of money you would otherwise finance through traditional lending vehicles, that cost may still be lower than application and origination fees for home equity or unsecured loans.*

The key is to evaluate the costs and options between traditional debt financing and investing your IRA/401(k) into the business. Make sure you understand the short-term and long-term costs of both, along with weighing whether or not to use your home as collateral or to deploy your retirement funds.

Either route you take exposes you to some amount of risk. That said, however, many entrepreneurs who choose to use their 401(k) for financing have concluded that they would rather owe money to themselves than to someone else.

Layered Financing

All the financing options we've described can be used in combination. The key is to employ them in a manner—and in the order—that works *for* you, not *against* you.

Often an entrepreneur sees an opportunity, gets excited by the possibilities (understandably, since the average entrepreneur is highly self-motivated), and becomes overzealous about financing. For example, let's say you locate a great opportunity and you want to purchase the business, so you quickly acquire an unsecured business loan. Then you seek an SBA loan—but now you have a maxed-out revolving-credit entry on your credit report. Consequently, your SBA loan is denied. So then you turn to home equity, but your lender is concerned about your credit utilization ratio as well as all the recent credit inquiries that show up on your credit report. *It can all snowball out of control if you don't take the first step carefully and wisely.*

Q & A

• Can I use funds from an individual IRA and roll those funds into a 401(k)?

You can roll funds from many different sources, including an IRA, 401(k) rollover, and 403(b). But you *cannot* roll a Roth IRA into this type of 401(k); if you have only a Roth IRA, you will not be able to use the retirement-fund strategy.

• Can I use retirement funds if I'm an absentee owner?

No. To place retirement funds into the company 401(k), you must be an eligible employee. An eligible employee is a person working in and for the business. If you plan to be a passive business owner instead of an active employee of the business, this type of financing is not appropriate.

• Can I establish an S corporation instead of a C corporation if I want to invest retirement funds?

No. Unfortunately, S corporations do not qualify for this strategy because the 410(k) plan is a shareholder, and under corporate law, all shareholders in an S corporation must be of "flesh and bone." In general terms, an S corporation can be considered an attractive business entity for tax purposes, because you can deduct losses against your personal income tax and there is no double tax on distributions. C corporations can be very effective tax-efficient business entities too. If you use the retirement-fund strategy, you will need to find a tax professional who can help you correctly use the benefits of a C corporation.

• Can I use my IRA or 401(k) as the 25 percent down payment for an SBA loan?

Yes. The SBA has created a proprietary process for this particular strategy. The process includes providing an exemption from the normal SBA guarantee requirements. The company you retain to create your 401(k) plan, in combination with your SBA lender, will help you navigate this process.

• Is investing my retirement funds legal, and what does the IRS think about this strategy?

Yes, investing your retirement funds into a small business is legal. There are explicit exemptions for these sorts of transactions in both the Internal Revenue Code and ERISA law. The IRS published an internal document called "Rollovers for Business Start-ups" in 2008. They did acknowledge the validity of this structure but were critical of how individuals operated them. For this reason, you must work with a company that has significant experience in facilitating and administering these kinds of plans.

• What do I need to do to qualify for the 401(k) investing vehicle?

First and most important, you must have sufficient funds in your 401(k) for the program to make sense. You should not consider this option unless you have at least $50,000 in your account. If you have less in your retirement plan, it is probably easier and cheaper (even including tax and penalties) to take a distribution instead. Then make sure you have a solid model and a great business plan—and never base your budgets on optimism alone.

• How long does it take to get traditional financing?

In our experience, *home equity loans* can typically be approved in approximately 30 days; the biggest variables are the appraisal, the qualification and underwriting process, and the lender's workload and willingness to turn the loan quickly. *SBA-guaranteed loans* can often take up to 90 days or more, depending on the level of documentation required.   The best way to shorten that time frame is to have your personal finances in order, with your documentation pulled together, including income, assets, financial statements, tax returns, W-2s, and so on. The faster you can provide the right information, the faster the loan can be processed. The time frames for *unsecured loans* vary widely and are largely dependent on your credit score and the amount of financing you need. The larger the loan, typically the longer the time frame, but in general terms, the average unsecured loan takes approximately 30 days to fund. *Peer-to-peer loan* time frames also vary; many platforms provide "automatic funding," which means that when enough micro-lenders participate to fund your request, those funds will be released.

• What types of collateral does the SBA typically prefer?

The best collateral is a secured asset that does not dramatically change in value. Real estate and other hard assets are usually preferred. The SBA may require up to 100 percent collateral for any loan granted.

✳ ✳ ✳

The bottom line is this: Do you believe in your business plan, your work ethic, and your skills? If you do, you'll need funding; your retirement plan could be an attractive option for that funding. Evaluate the options, weigh each possibility carefully, and make the choice that's right for *you*.

Investing Retirement Funds: Paul's Story

Paul followed a savvy business strategy when he purchased a small storage facility in 2005. Paul had retired earlier that year after three decades with a state agriculture department, and he knew that he wanted to do something different. He was one of the growing numbers of individuals who use their retirement funds to start their company.

The first storage unit that Paul purchased had a companion business as part of it that appeared to be slightly unconventional to him at the time: it also sold cell phones and cell phone plans for a start-up company, US Cellular. He and his wife were initially dubious as to whether this additional business would be a match for them, but it exceeded their expectations. When they acquired their second storage facility, they immediately began offering US Cellular there, too.

Both sides of the business have grown. They have at times had 100 percent occupancy, and the phone business now makes almost as much as the mini-storage facilities.

Paul has learned that it is possible to run two unrelated businesses under the same roof. The shared overhead is a great benefit, and he loves the diversification.

Paul's experience also exemplifies successful investment of retirement funds into an entrepreneurial venture. Retirement funds gave him the financial underpinning to launch the business, and the business, in turn, is proving to be a sound investment in his future.

Risk and Fear

"To act is to be committed, and to be committed is to be in danger."

—James Baldwin

In Chapter 1 we referred to the "twin demons" of risk and fear. And, indeed, these two factors stop many potential entrepreneurs in their tracks. Here we examine them more closely and suggest ways to develop a realistic perspective so that your entrepreneurial dreams don't become nightmares.

What Is Risk?

Risk is defined as exposure to a chance of loss or damage. Risk is something we deal with every day. When you get in your car, you risk being in an accident. When you eat at a restaurant, you risk getting food poisoning. Risk is everywhere. A small business can be extremely rewarding, but it also has risks: you might never turn a profit, go out of business, and be forced to file bankruptcy.

There is no doubt that we assume more risk as an employer than we do as an employee. But entrepreneurs understand and embrace risk. They have a unique relationship with risk. They understand that without risk there is little reward.

Another way to approach this is to consider the question: Who is in control? Entrepreneurs believe that if they are in control, there is a greater likelihood of success. They are calculated risk takers. The reason we advise people to look at many businesses, get appraisals, use a team of advisors, and build a solid, well-thought-out business plan is to mitigate the risk to the entrepreneur and to shift risk from a position of fear to one of confidence or faith.

If other people hire you, it is because they realize your talents will contribute to the success of their organization, you will contribute to their dream. They are willing to invest up front to cover your costs until you contribute in a meaningful way to their venture. To go into business for yourself, you have to believe enough in your own abilities to take on risk so you can personally realize the true value of your talents. It's an investment in yourself, in your dream.

Confidence is the key element in dealing with risk. Why would you take a job if you thought you would fail? What is the difference if you consider "hiring" yourself? The only roadblocks are your own limiting beliefs.

What Is Fear?

"The best measure of courage is the fear that is overcome."
—Norman F. Dixon, Psychologist and Author

We all have fears. Fear is a natural reaction to not having knowledge. We fear the unknown. "What happens if …?" It's the question that torments us all—including those who are thinking about becoming an entrepreneur.

Like marathon runners, individuals considering their own business often come upon a "wall." In a marathon, it is usually about 18 miles into the race; in a business venture, it often takes hold a few days before you have to sign a bank commitment, lease, or franchise agreement. It is the ability to overcome the fear, to push yourself beyond what you thought was possible, that will make the biggest difference in whether you achieve your goal.

Fear manifests itself in many ways. For example, there once was a very bright and financially savvy client who said he feared losing everything and having to live with his mother. That fear was very real to that particular client until we talked it through and could not come up with a rational circumstance where that would happen. He moved forward with his business.

One way to build the courage to face your fears is by imagining yourself in the situations you fear and reasoning through the possible outcomes, as our client did. What if you strike out to reach your dreams and fail? What if you never pursue your dreams and one day realize your life is about over and it's too late? Which would be worse? Is not trying something a success? How we define failure can often dictate our fear. If reaching a "final goal" were the only motivation and measure of success, then most ventures might be considered failures.

Knowledge diminishes fear. If you find yourself feeling anxious, ask more questions. Spend time getting to the root of your fear; then get answers. We are better able to make good decisions when we obtain factual information. When you are pursuing or evaluating small business ownership, ask questions to alleviate most of the natural anxiety you feel. Fearing the unknown and letting it paralyze you causes inaction and failure.

Preparation also diminishes fear. Think through questions such as these: If you lost your job today, what would happen? Would you start a business or look for another job? If you had enough savings to live on for a year, would you leave your job and focus on your dream of being an entrepreneur? How about enough savings for two years, or three years? Where is your threshold? How much is enough? If you can pinpoint the minimum safety net that would push you to choose your dreams, work to build your savings to that level. If you cannot imagine any reasonable amount that would make you feel comfortable, that is an early indication that a job working for someone else may be best—especially if you see a business as an expense rather than an investment.

It's important to realize that overcoming fear is something that needs ongoing attention. Some business owners run successful businesses for many years and suddenly experience challenges from the economy, changing trends, regulatory issues, or possibly their health. There are unexpected setbacks related to employees quitting, losses of customers and accounts, mistakes, competitor actions, new discoveries, and on and on. Many of these seasoned and successful entrepreneurs have gained great knowledge and experiences, supported their families and became very wealthy, yet they had to successfully manage through their fears to maintain the dream. In business as in life, the only thing you can count on is change, and entrepreneurs deal promptly with those challenges that surface.

By constantly seeking new knowledge to develop and improve your skills, you will be able to respond to most situations. This type of confidence feeds upon itself, and you become more powerful after facing each event.

Thus you must be flexible, receptive to new information, decisive, and take action to solve problems. In addition to collecting the right information to make the best decisions and take action, you must also be ready to take responsibility for your actions.

While this might seem like a daunting prospect to the employee who has coworkers, a boss, and a paycheck to rely on, facing your fears without this kind of safety net and emerging victorious can be far more exhilarating than the rewards most employees will ever receive.

In our own personal situations, both of us would have considered it a failure to spend a life working for others without the freedom to reap the rewards of our efforts by taking control of our fate. Being haunted by the question of "what if I had tried?" would have been too much to bear.

So remember the simple fact that the fear of following your dreams is based on the fear of the unknown. When you have the skills, the resources, the plans, a support group of peers and mentors, and unrelenting persistence, nothing will stop you.

Accepting Risks and Overcoming Fear: Don and Kent's Story

Entrepreneurs Don and Kent, founders of the first distillery in Washington State since Prohibition, haven't come up "dry" in terms of their success—their first whiskey release sold out in 90 minutes. After just three years, their products are now available in 18 states and three countries. And to top it off, their distillery won "best vodka" and "double gold medal" awards for its Washington State Wheat Vodka at a World Spirit Competition—beating out Grey Goose, Belvedere, and others!

Like many entrepreneurs, their success was in no way assured, however, even though the partners had significant business experience. "Kent and I both were in the food business," says Don. "I was the director of marketing for a large food company. Kent worked for a food distributor in Minnesota as vice president of merchandising and marketing. I think we both hit terminal corporate burnout within about a week of one another."

After further research, Don put together a business plan, ran it by Kent, and asked if he wanted to be an investor. "Instead of just investing," Don says, "Kent said, 'Why don't I just do it with you?' The rest is history."

To gain the knowledge they needed, the small-business owners studied with Kris Berglund, who established the Artisan Distilling Program at Michigan State University, and they trained at distilleries in Germany. Their learning curve was steep, but their success curve was equally steep.

So what were the entrepreneurs' biggest concerns when they started their small business? Don admits, "Our biggest fears at the beginning were: Can we make a product the market is going to come to? Can we compete? Do we have enough knowledge to run a small business and make it work?" Of course, it turns out that the answers to those questions were "yes" in all cases. But without overcoming their initial fears, they might never have undertaken the venture in the first place.

Don also offers advice for potential entrepreneurs who dream of starting or buying a small business. "I'm a voracious planner, so I think detailed planning to the nth degree is really important. Having a business plan that creates a blueprint for what you actually plan on doing is an important aspect. Then I think you just have to have what I call 'entrepreneurial blindness,' where you're all in, you're going, and failure is not an option."

Section IV:
Parting Thoughts

13

The Nature of Entrepreneurs

Are entrepreneurs kamikaze pilots willing to risk the family fortune or future? Are they adrenalin-pumped, deal-worshipping junkies who cannot work for someone else? Do they buy the parts to the glider and build it after they jump off the cliff? Some do, but that is not the individual to whom we have addressed this book.

We wrote this book because we believe in the American dream of entrepreneurship. The dream exists and is the path to economic security for individuals, families, cities, states, and our country. It is our combined dream that we have given you additional tools with which to make the journey to self-reliance.

In this book we have tried to educate you on how hardworking individuals can break the bond of working for someone else—and why they should do so. On an intellectual level, it would seem like an easy task: get an idea, organize financials, develop a plan, launch a business, and work as hard as you would for anyone else.

You certainly would not be the first to pursue this vision—especially given the reality that most employees rarely develop significant wealth or a lifestyle that is focused on what is important to them and their families. Do you accept the fact that most of the wealth in this country is held by people who run small businesses? Have you realized, as we stated at the outset, that working for other people helps them to realize *their* dream, not yours; that wealth is accumulated by owning equity and that people who work for a salary usually live at the level of their compensation and don't have nearly enough left over for savings? Retirement plans are subject to ebbs and flows that could wreak havoc on your individual time frame to financial security. So why does the chasm between a job and entrepreneurship appear so wide and untraversable? It certainly can't be that the alternative—working for another's dream—is that attractive.

Although we can't cite the exact reference, we believe it is intuitively correct to assume that a high percentage of the working population would like to be in their own business or at least want to enjoy the rewards of freedom, independence, and financial security that come with a successful commercial venture. How can we change that dream into an action plan?

First, it is important to resist the tendency to let initial perceptions and assumptions control your thinking. And, as we have discussed in depth in earlier chapters, fear plays a big role in those perceptions and assumptions. A "no" answer is so much safer than "yes," particularly if you think short term. After working with hundreds of entrepreneur dreamers, we still find it amazing how often they let their fears overpower their dreams.

And so we repeat our earlier point that the most important step you can take in controlling your own destiny is to manage your fears—which, we acknowledge is not an easy task. We all are wired in a fight-or-flight mode when we feel a threat to our security, and an entrepreneurial venture, if not well planned or considered, can certainly seem like a threat to your economic well-being rather than a move toward self-reliance. It seems much safer to do nothing than to risk capital and time in a business venture.

14

Questions and Answers

In a final effort to help you dispel your fears, we offer here examples of rationalizations that may sound familiar to you. They're the kinds of statements we often hear from individuals who are still struggling to find the courage to pursue their vision, and the replies are what a good entrepreneurial coach would say in response.

"It is not the right time."

> When is the right time? If you wait for a recession to be over or for the news to report a booming economy, it may be too late and someone else will have taken your idea and already be off and running. What circumstances create a "right time"? Are you analyzing the opportunity objectively? By saying it is not the right time, are you avoiding responsibility?

"What if I fail?"

> If I were offering you a job, would you have the same level of concern about failing? What is the difference? Is it relating to who is taking the risk, you or me? Have you

considered the relationship between risk and reward? Do you realize that I can terminate your working relationship with me at my will? Your work history is one of success and achievement. What makes you think that would stop just because you are doing it for yourself?

"What if no one buys my product or service?"
Let's talk about the circumstances where that could happen. What assumptions are considered in your business plan? What are the potential risks and how would you handle them if they were to occur? Is this a rational fear, given what you know about the market and the current suppliers?

"I hear that owning a business is a 24-hour commitment and you give up your life."
What do you want it to be? Will you work *in* the business as a technician or *on* the business as a visionary? I suggest that you read *The E-Myth Revisited* by Michael Gerber to better understand how your relationship to your company can influence its success.

"What if there is another recession?"
Will macroeconomics affect your life? Only if you let it! Would your job be more secure, or future job prospects better, in a lingering recession? If you chose a recession-resistant business, what happens when all boats start to rise during a growth economy? It is very difficult to time things that are out of your control. One could argue that starting a business during a recession is the *best* time. Interest rates are low, leases are more negotiable, equipment is cheaper, employees are more available, and buyers are always looking for better, cheaper, faster solutions.

15

Your Turn to Make the Jump

"The best years of your life are the ones in which you decide your problems are your own ... you realize you control your own destiny."

—Albert Ellis, Psychologist and Author

The excuses for not starting a business are as wide and varied as creativity itself. When you boil it down, you can no longer afford to bury your head in the sand. Your time on this earth is like gold; it goes up in value as it becomes a limited commodity. *Now* is the right time to begin a serious, calculated, and intentional effort to become an entrepreneur. You may be the best auto mechanic, sign maker, baker, wine connoisseur, or computer wizard. All we are saying is that you will excel when you are working for yourself and are motivated to use your business to achieve the most important things you want in your life.

To sum up our efforts at educating, motivating, and perhaps putting a little fear in you about staying on the same old path, here is a reiteration of our key ideas.

Create a vision for what you want your life to be like, including financial and lifestyle goals. Find a need that people will pay for, and consider it your mission to fill it. Spend ample time in developing your business plans, including your underlying assumptions and financial implications. Be patient but intentional.

There is a point in life where we must stop "getting ready to get ready." Believe in yourself and take an educated leap. Figure out who you are, what you love, and who you really want to be—and then decide what fits in your personal plan so that you can be happy.

Each of us is presented with paths throughout life. Each trail is a choice of direction that will deliver us to a different destination. Our choices are determined by our past, our environment and influences, and our desires, courage, and fears. We can cling to the familiar course and only surmise what might have been, or we can take at least one step toward a new venture.

Entrepreneurship begins with an ounce of inspiration and a pound of courage. It is a journey taken by many in pursuit of their most important personal objectives and visions.

If you follow their example, you'll be on your way to fulfilling your own ambitions and taking your place among the millions of successful entrepreneurs who've made the jump and never looked back.

About the Authors

Jeff Levy is an entrepreneur, coach, and mentor who helps people clarify their goals and values so they can properly evaluate self-employment career options. Through his coaching business, which is part of a well-respected national organization of coaches, he has helped countless individuals begin their road to self-employment and has participated in more than 100 franchise start-ups. In 2009 he was nominated as coach of the year by The Entrepreneur's Source®. His personal experiences with assorted entrepreneurial ventures are highlighted in the book *Changing Careers After 40,* by Terry Pile and David Lingle.

Jeff was previously Vice President of Marketing for Source Kramer Corp, a Seattle-area start-up, and President and COO of Spider Staging Corporation before it was acquired by Flow International Corporation. Following the acquisition, he became VP Marketing for Flow International and then a partner and Executive Vice President of Safeworks, LLC.

Jeff is past chairman of the educational committee at the Seattle University Business School Entrepreneurship Center and serves on its board.

David Nilssen is a serial entrepreneur and is recognized as a leading expert on small business and franchise finance. He has spoken at hundreds of domestic and international events since starting a business to help aspiring entrepreneurs find the capital they need for their small business or franchise. David has helped nearly 5,000 individuals invest nearly $2 billion into small businesses or franchises, creating more than 50,000 American jobs and generating hundreds of millions in economic output. David founded his current business in 2003 with less than $10,000 and a laptop, eventually transforming it into an Inc 500 organization with thousands of clients in all 50 states and generating over $50 million in revenues. Along the way, he and his firm have been recognized by many industry and civic organizations, such as *Inc Magazine* (appearing on the Inc 5000 list 2008–2010) and the US Chamber of Commerce (NW Regional Small Business of the Year, 2007). Also in 2007, the Small Business Administration (SBA) named Nilssen the National Young Entrepreneur of the Year.

David serves on the boards of the Entrepreneur Organization and Youth Ventures.